42 Days to

A Stronger

Marriage

A Christ-Centered Devotional for Couples

Daniel Moore

Connecting the Gap Ministries

To my amazing wife, Michelle

You are my greatest earthly blessing and, once again, the heartbeat behind this devotional.

Your love, faith, and grace inspire me daily to be a better husband and follower of Christ.

Through every season, joyful and challenging, you've shown what it means to build a marriage rooted in God's Word and strengthened by His love.

This book is a reflection of the journey we've shared and the faithfulness of the God who holds us together.

Thank you for walking beside me, praying with me, and believing in the mission God placed in our hearts.

With all my love,
Daniel

CONTENTS

PREFACE

Marriage is one of God's most beautiful creations, a covenant designed not just for companionship, but for purpose. When a husband and wife commit to love each other as Christ loves the Church, their union becomes a living testimony of God's grace, forgiveness, and faithfulness.

Yet even the strongest marriages face challenges. Life gets busy, hearts drift, and the fire that once burned bright can grow dim. Over time, couples can find themselves living under the same roof but not truly walking hand in hand, spiritually, emotionally, or physically.

That's why *42 Days to a Stronger Marriage* was written. It's more than just a devotional, it's an intentional journey for couples who desire to reconnect with each other and, most importantly, with Christ. Over these forty-two days, you and your spouse will be encouraged to pray together, reflect on God's Word, and take small, practical steps that lead to lasting transformation.

Each day is designed to strengthen your faith, deepen your intimacy, and remind you that a thriving marriage doesn't happen by accident, it's built one Christ-centered choice at a time. Whether your relationship is in a season of joy or in need of healing, God's truth has the power to renew and restore.

My prayer is that as you journey through these pages, you'll experience a fresh outpouring of God's presence in your marriage. May your love grow stronger, your communication deeper, and your unity more unshakable than ever before.

Together, let's rediscover the joy of doing marriage God's way — because when Christ is at the center, everything else finds its proper place.

Acknowledgements

First and foremost, I give all glory and honor to **God**, the Author and Sustainer of marriage. Without His grace, wisdom, and unfailing love, none of this would be possible. Every word in these pages is a reflection of His goodness and the truth found in His Word. To Him be all the praise for every life and marriage He touches through this devotional.

To my incredible wife, **Michelle,** thank you for being my partner in life, love, and ministry. Your patience, encouragement, and unwavering faith have strengthened me more than words can express. You live out the message of a Christ-centered marriage every single day, and I am endlessly grateful for your love and the way you make our marriage a reflection of Christ's love for the Church.

To our **children, their spouses, and grandchildren**, you are God's beautiful legacy in our lives. Each of you reminds us daily of His faithfulness through generations. May you always see in us an example of imperfect people clinging to a perfect Savior and learning to love through His strength.

And to all the **listeners of the Marriage Life and More Podcast** and the **Connecting the Gap Podcast,** thank you for your continued support, your prayers, and your hunger to grow in your walk with Christ. Your stories, feedback, and encouragement inspire me to keep creating and sharing resources that help strengthen faith and family.

Finally, to **everyone** who picks up this book, thank you. My prayer is that the words within these pages point you to Christ and inspire you to live out God's beautiful design in your life, relationships, and your marriages.

From my heart to yours, thank you for being a part of this journey. My prayer is that this devotional helps you draw closer to your spouse and to the God who designed marriage for His glory and our joy.

WEEK ONE

DAYS 1-7

THEME:
GOD'S DESIGN FOR MARRIAGE: THE FOUNDATION

KEY VERSE: GENESIS 2:24

Therefore a man shall leave his father and his mother and hold fast to his wife, and they shall become one flesh

Day One

Marriage: God's Idea, Not Ours

Scripture: *Genesis 2:18–25 (ESV) — "Therefore a man shall leave his father and his mother and hold fast to his wife, and they shall become one flesh."*

In a quiet village surrounded by mountains, an old clockmaker named Tobias was known for building the finest timepieces. People came from far and wide to see how each clock ticked in perfect harmony, every gear designed with purpose, each part fitting exactly where it belonged.

One day, a young couple visited Tobias and asked him to create a special clock for their wedding gift. While working on it, Tobias told them a story.

'You know,' he said as he carefully fit the gears together, 'marriage is like this clock. It looks simple from the outside, but the inside is a carefully planned design. And just like I didn't invent how these gears should turn together, man didn't invent marriage. It was God's idea from the very beginning.'

He paused and looked up.

'Genesis tells us that it was God who said, "It is not good for the man to be alone; I will make a helper suitable for him." God didn't leave humans to figure it out. He gave us marriage as a gift and a picture of His own love.'

The couple watched closely as Tobias set the final piece in place. The clock began to tick steadily, gently, and in perfect rhythm.

'If you try to build it without the design of the Creator,' he said, 'everything falls out of sync. But when you follow His plan, every part moves together in harmony.'

Marriage didn't begin in a courtroom or culture — it started in a garden. Marriage is not a man-made concept, nor is it a cultural convenience. It is a divine creation, a sacred design authored by God Himself. When we view marriage through that lens, everything changes. It's not just about compatibility or companionship, it's about covenant. Just as the clockmaker in the story didn't randomly assemble gears but followed a precise design, God intentionally crafted marriage to reflect His own nature: unity, love, and purpose.

In Genesis 2:18, God says, 'It is not good for the man to be alone; I will make a helper suitable for him.' This wasn't a reaction to Adam's loneliness — it was a declaration of divine purpose. God wasn't just solving a problem; He was unveiling a plan. Marriage was His idea from the very beginning, designed to mirror the relationship within the Trinity and to show the world what faithful, sacrificial love looks like.

When we forget that marriage is God's design, we risk reducing it to a contract based on feelings or circumstances. But when we remember that it is a covenant rooted in God's heart, we begin to treat it with the reverence it deserves. We approach it with humility, knowing we are stewards of something holy. We approach it with hope, trusting that the One who designed it is also the One who empowers us to live it out.

The illustration of the clock is a powerful reminder: every part has a place, every movement has a purpose, and when aligned with the Creator's design, the result is harmony. In the same way, when we build our marriages according to God's blueprint, we experience unity that goes beyond emotion — it becomes spiritual alignment.

> Your marriage is not an accident. It's a divine assignment. God placed you and your spouse together not just for your happiness, but for your holiness. He is using your relationship to shape you into the image of Christ. That means even the hard and challenging moments have purpose. Even the seasons of silence or struggle are opportunities for growth, grace, and deeper unity.

So today, don't just look at your spouse as your partner, see them as a gift from God, entrusted to you for His glory. And don't just try to make your marriage work, invite God to be the center of it. He is the Master Designer, and when He is at the heart of your union, every tick, every turn, every season can move in perfect harmony. If He authored your story, He can also sustain it.

Reflection Question:

How would your daily attitude toward your spouse change if you viewed your marriage as a sacred calling rather than a personal choice?

Couples Challenge:

Pray together today, thanking God for writing your love story. Say out loud to each other, "Our marriage belongs to God."

Prayer:

Lord, thank You for designing marriage with such purpose and beauty. Remind us that You are the Author and Sustainer of our relationship. Teach us to see our covenant through Your eyes and to walk in unity and grace. Amen.

Day Two

The Purpose of Oneness

Scripture: *Ecclesiastes 4:9–12 (ESV) — "Two are better than one, because they have a good reward for their toil."*

There was a young couple, Brandon and Grace, who had been married for just a few years. At first, their love felt effortless. But as life moved on, bills piled up, their toddler tested every ounce of patience, and their once-easy conversations turned into tense debates, they began to feel like they were pulling in opposite directions.

Brandon liked to plan everything in detail. Grace preferred to be spontaneous. He was quiet when struggling; she needed to talk things through. Eventually, they started seeing each other's differences as problems rather than gifts. Every conversation became a competition. Who was right, who tried harder, who understood more. The love was still there, but it was buried under weariness and unspoken frustration.

One evening, after a particularly hard week, they sat on the porch in silence. The tension between them could be felt.

Finally, Grace broke the quiet. 'Why does it feel like we're always fighting each other instead of fighting for us?'

Brandon thought about it. Then quietly replied, 'Because somewhere along the way, we forgot we're on the same team.'

From that evening on, they made a decision, not to fix each other or compete with each other, but to cooperate and move forward together. It wasn't always perfect, but each time they chose unity over pride, peace would follow.

They learned that oneness didn't mean being alike, it meant working in harmony. Brandon's planning helped them stay grounded. Grace's spontaneity brought joy to their routine. Their differences no longer divided them; they strengthened what they were building.

Oneness in marriage is not about being identical — it's about being intentional. God never meant for couples to be carbon copies of each other. Instead, He brings together two uniquely designed people to form something more substantial, more complete, and more beautiful than either could be alone. Just like Brandon and Grace learned, unity doesn't mean uniformity. It means embracing each other's strengths and weaknesses, and choosing to move forward together, even when it's difficult.

Ecclesiastes 4:9 says, 'Two are better than one, because they have a good return for their labor.' This verse reminds us that God created marriage to be a partnership, not a rivalry. When we stop trying to win individual battles and start fighting for the relationship, we experience the power of true oneness. That kind of unity doesn't happen by accident — it's a daily decision. It's choosing to listen when you'd rather argue. It's choosing to forgive when it would be easier to hold a grudge. It's choosing to believe the best about each other, even in moments of frustration.

> The enemy loves to use division to weaken what God has joined. He whispers lies like, 'You're too different,' or 'They'll never understand you.' But every time you respond with grace, patience, and humility, you're pushing back against that scheme. You're declaring, 'We're not opponents—we're allies.'

Brandon's structure and Grace's spontaneity were never meant to compete — they were meant to complement. In the same way, your differences with your spouse are not obstacles to overcome but opportunities to grow. When you start seeing your spouse's uniqueness as a gift rather than a frustration, your marriage begins to reflect the creativity and unity of God Himself.

So today, take time to remember you're on the same team. Whether you're navigating parenting challenges, financial stress, or emotional disconnect, you're not alone. God is with you, and He's given you each other, not to compete, but to complete. Don't let pride or pressure pull you apart. Choose unity. Choose grace. Choose to pull in the same direction. That's where peace and purpose begin to flourish.

Reflection Question:

Where are you most tempted to pull in opposite directions right now, and how could unity look in that area?

Couples Challenge:

Do one task *together* today, cook, pray, or plan something, and remind yourselves, "We're better together."

Prayer:

Father, thank You for the gift of unity. Help us see our marriage through Your design of teamwork and trust. When division tries to creep in, anchor us in Your peace and purpose. Amen.

Day Three

Reflecting Christ's Love

Scripture: *Ephesians 5:32–33 (ESV) — "This mystery is profound, and I am saying that it refers to Christ and the church."*

Jonathan and Rachel had been married for over a decade. On the surface, their life looked like anyone else's, two kids, steady jobs, a mortgage that never seemed to shrink, and a calendar filled with school events and grocery runs. But beneath the routine, something sacred quietly unfolded in the ordinary.

There was the night Jonathan came home tense and weary, the day's frustrations still clinging to him like dust. Rachel had already endured her own battles, sick kids, piles of laundry, and a kitchen that never seemed to stay clean. The air between them thickened with unspoken exhaustion. For a moment, irritation threatened to speak first.

Then Rachel simply reached out, laid a hand on his arm, and said softly, "Let's just sit for a bit."

It wasn't dramatic, but it was a reset of the atmosphere. That gentle pause, born of patience and love, shifted the entire evening. They sat in silence, shoulders touching, the quiet stronger than any argument could have been.

Another morning told a similar story. Rachel had overslept, and the house was in chaos, shoes missing, lunches forgotten, everyone running late. Frustration flared, and she snapped at Jonathan. He could have snapped back. Instead, he took a quiet breath, packed the kids' lunches, and kissed her forehead before walking out the door.

Hours later, her text came through: *"I'm sorry. Thank you for showing me grace."*

There were no grand gestures or public displays of perfection, just steady, unseen acts of love. Moments when pride could have spoken, but grace did instead. Over time, those choices built something far more substantial than fleeting romance: a marriage that mirrored the love they both had come to know from the One who first showed them how to love.

It wasn't flawless. It was faithful. And in the quiet rhythm of everyday life, Jonathan and Rachel's marriage became a reflection of something eternal, love that gives, forgives, and endures.

Paul said in Ephesians 5:32-33 that marriage is a mystery pointing to Christ and His Church. Jonathan and Rachel didn't love each other perfectly, but through every act of faithfulness, patience, and kindness, they reflected something holy. Their home became a quiet message to their children, their friends, and even their neighbors: this is what Jesus' love looks like. Not flashy, not flawless, but faithful.

Marriage, at its core, is not just about two people building a life together, it's about two people becoming a living picture of the gospel. Ephesians 5:32–33 reminds us that this union is a mystery pointing to Christ and the Church. That means every ordinary moment, every act of love, patience, and forgiveness, carries eternal weight. Jonathan and Rachel's story show us that the most powerful displays of God's love often happen in the quiet, unseen moments, when grace is chosen over retaliation, when kindness replaces frustration, and when humility bridges the gap between two hearts.

> The beauty of gospel-centered marriage isn't found in perfection — it's found in reflection. You don't have to have flawless communication or a conflict-free home to honor God in your marriage. What matters is that you keep turning toward grace. Every time you choose to forgive when it's hard, to serve when you feel tired, to speak gently when you're frustrated, you are preaching the gospel without words. You are showing what Jesus' love looks like in real time.

This kind of love teaches your children how to be patient and kind. It shows your friends that forgiveness is possible. It tells your neighbors that something holy is happening behind your front door, even if it's not flashy or polished. That's the power of a marriage rooted in Christ—it becomes a daily testimony of faithfulness, not just between two people, but between God and His people.

So, if you feel like your marriage is too ordinary to matter, remember this: the gospel is often most clearly seen in the ordinary. In the small acts of selflessness. In the quiet apologies. In the daily commitment to love again. That's where Jesus shows up. And that's where your marriage becomes more than a relationship — it becomes a reflection of heaven's love on earth. Keep choosing grace. Keep choosing each other. That's the mystery. That's the gospel.

Reflection Question:

What does your marriage currently reflect to those watching? What might need to change to better display Christ's love?

Couples Challenge:

Ask each other, "How can I love you more like Jesus this week?" Then do one small act that shows that love.

Prayer:

Jesus, teach us to love each other the way You have loved us, sacrificially, patiently, and faithfully. Let our marriage be a mirror of Your grace to everyone who sees it. Amen.

Day Four

Covenant vs. Contract

Scripture: *Malachi 2:14–16 (ESV) — "But you say, "Why does he not?" Because the Lord was witness between you and the wife of your youth, to whom you have been faithless, though she is your companion and your wife by covenant."*

Jack and Eliza stood on the porch of their weathered farmhouse, twenty-seven years into a marriage that had felt the full weight of real life. The white paint had long since begun to peel, the boards creaking beneath their feet, small reminders of the years they'd stood through together. Their story wasn't one of ease or perfection, but of choosing, over and over again, to stay.

Early in their marriage, the storms came hard. Jack lost his job, and with it, much of his confidence. Bills piled up, tension rose, and the laughter that once filled their home grew scarce. Conversations turned sharp, then silent. One night, worn down and uncertain, Jack packed a bag. He wasn't running from Eliza — he was running from the weight of disappointment he didn't know how to carry.

When he reached the door, Eliza was there waiting. Her eyes were tired, her voice low but steady.

"I don't need everything to be fixed," she said. "I just need *us*. Even if we're bruised, even if we're not sure what's next, I'm not giving up."

That moment changed the direction of their story. The problems didn't vanish, but something stronger took root, an understanding that their marriage was not a contract that could be canceled when it got hard, but a covenant they had entered before God. It wasn't about convenience. It was about faithfulness.

Over the years, they would face more losses, misunderstandings, and long nights of silence followed by mornings of slow reconciliation. But they also discovered joy, quiet mornings with coffee and laughter over small things, shared prayers whispered in the dark, and the deep peace that comes when you know someone has truly chosen you, again and again.

Their marriage wasn't flawless, but it was sacred. What held them together wasn't the absence of conflict, but the presence of commitment, a love that said, *even when it's hard, even when it hurts, I'm staying.*

Jack and Eliza's story became a living picture of covenant love, two imperfect people held together not by circumstance, but by promise. The kind of love that endures not because it's easy, but because it's the way God created it to be.

Jack and Eliza's story remind us that marriage is not held together by feelings or flawless seasons — it's held together by faithfulness. Malachi 2:14–16 speaks to the seriousness with which God views marriage. He calls it a covenant, not a contract. A covenant is a sacred promise, witnessed by God, rooted not in convenience but in commitment.

In today's culture, it's easy to treat relationships like contracts: agreements that last only as long as both parties meet certain conditions. But God's design for marriage is deeper. Contracts say, 'I'll stay as long as you make me happy.' Covenants say, 'I'll stay even when I'm hurting, even when we're struggling, because I made a promise — before God and to you.'

This kind of love mirrors God's own faithfulness to us. He doesn't walk away when we fail. He doesn't withdraw His love when we're at our worst. He stays. He forgives. He rebuilds. And He calls us to reflect that same kind of love in our marriages.

> When we treat marriage like a covenant, we stop keeping score and start offering grace. We stop asking, 'What do I get out of this?' and start asking, 'How can I love well today?' Covenant love doesn't mean ignoring pain or pretending everything is fine, it means staying present through the pain, choosing to rebuild when it would be easier to run, and leaning on God's strength when your own runs out.

Jack and Eliza's perseverance didn't come from having all the answers or never failing each other. It came from choosing, again and again, to stay. To forgive. To press on. That's the kind of love that lasts. That's the kind of love that reflects God's heart.

So, if you're walking through a hard season in your marriage, remember this: God doesn't call you to perfection — He calls you to perseverance. He honors the couple who choose covenant over comfort, who cling to each other when everything else says to let go. And in that faithfulness, He writes a story that is not only beautiful, but also holy.

Reflection Question:

In what ways can you honor your marriage covenant more intentionally this week?

Couples Challenge:

Write or say one thing to your spouse today that reminds them, "I'm committed to you, no matter what."

Prayer:

God, thank You for teaching us what covenant love looks like through Your faithfulness. Strengthen our commitment and help us love beyond convenience or condition. Amen.

DAY FIVE

Building on the Rock

Scripture: *Matthew 7:24–27 (ESV) — "And the rain fell, and the floods came, and the winds blew and beat on that house, but it did not fall, because it had been founded on the rock."*

Mark and Jenna had been married six years when the storm hit. Not the kind that rattles windows or floods streets, but the kind that shakes a marriage from the inside out.

It began when Mark lost his job. What was supposed to be a short setback stretched into months of uncertainty. Around the same time, Jenna's mother was diagnosed with cancer, and her days were filled with doctor visits and late-night worry. Bills piled up, patience wore thin, and their once-light conversations turned into short tempers and long silences.

The cracks began to show, not in their home, but in their hearts. What once felt steady now felt fragile. One night, after another tense argument, Jenna sat on the edge of their bed and whispered, "How did we get here?"

Mark didn't know. But the question lingered. A few days later, while sitting alone in the living room, he reached for his Bible, the same one that had gathered dust on the shelf for months. As he read, he was reminded of a truth he had long forgotten, storms are inevitable, but collapse isn't — if what you're building on is solid.

That thought stayed with him. When he shared it with Jenna, something softened between them. They both realized that much of their marriage had been built on things that shifted, feelings, routines, expectations. They had forgotten the foundation that once held them steady.

So, they began again, not with grand gestures, but small, intentional choices. Morning coffee together with a short prayer. Reading Scripture before making big decisions. Choosing forgiveness instead of defensiveness. Reaching for each other's hand even when frustration lingered.

The circumstances didn't suddenly improve. The job didn't appear overnight. Jenna's mom's illness still weighed heavily. But something in *them* began to change. Fear no longer dictated their days. The tension in their home slowly gave way to peace, one quiet act of faith at a time.

Years later, when they looked back on that season, they didn't remember it as the time everything fell apart, but as the time they learned how to build something that could last.

Because the truth is, any marriage can stand tall in the sunshine. But when the storms come, and they always do, only those built on something unshakable will remain standing.

Mark and Jenna's story is a powerful reminder that storms are not a sign of failure, they're a part of life. Jesus never promised that the rain wouldn't fall or that the winds wouldn't blow. What He promised was that the house built on the rock would not fall. That truth applies just as much to marriage as it does to individual lives.

Every couple will face seasons of hardship, whether it's financial strain, health crises, emotional distance, or spiritual dryness. The question isn't whether storms will come, but whether your marriage is built on something strong enough to withstand them. When emotions run high and circumstances feel overwhelming, what you've built on will be revealed.

Jesus says in Matthew 7:24–27 that the wise man is the one who hears His words and puts them into practice. That means the strength of your marriage isn't measured by how good it looks in calm weather, but by how deeply it's rooted in God's Word. If your foundation is built on feelings, assumptions, or cultural expectations, the pressure of life will eventually expose the cracks. But if your foundation is God's truth, His promises, His commands, His grace, then even the fiercest storm can't shake you.

Mark and Jenna didn't find a quick fix. Their circumstances didn't change overnight. But when they began to build on the Word through prayer, Scripture, honesty, and forgiveness, they began to experience peace in the middle of the storm. That's what happens when you choose obedience over pride, prayer over panic, and forgiveness over resentment. Each of those choices is like laying another stone on the Rock.

So, ask yourself today: What are you building your marriage on? Is it your own strength, your spouse's mood, or the shifting winds of circumstance? Or is it the unchanging truth of God's Word? When Scripture becomes your foundation, your marriage doesn't just survive the storm — it grows stronger through it.

You don't need a perfect marriage to stand firm. You need a faithful foundation. Keep building, even when it's hard. Keep trusting, even when it's slow. Because when the storm passes, and it will, you'll still be standing, not because of your strength, but because you built on the Rock.

Reflection Question:

What's one "sand foundation" you might be trusting in instead of God's truth?

Couples Challenge:

Read a short passage together tonight (start with Psalm 127) and pray, "Lord, be the foundation of our home."

Prayer:

Lord Jesus, help us build our marriage on Your truth. Teach us to live by Your Word and rely on Your strength when storms come. Amen.

Day Six

Inviting God Into the Center

Scripture: *Colossians 3:17 (ESV) — "And whatever you do, in word or deed, do everything in the name of the Lord Jesus, giving thanks to God the Father through him."*

Lena and Chris had been married for almost ten years. They loved each other, truly, but somewhere between the demands of work, parenting, and the endless to-do lists, something quiet had shifted. Their lives were full, yet their hearts felt half-empty.

They still did all the "right things", church on Sundays, grace before meals, a quick prayer when life felt uncertain, but the closeness they once shared with God, and with each other, had begun to fade into the background. What used to be a partnership of faith had slowly become a routine of survival.

One evening, after a small argument over something neither of them would remember the next day, Lena sat at the kitchen table long after Chris had gone to bed. The hum of the refrigerator was the only sound in the room. Staring at the dim light above the sink, she whispered, "God, when did we stop walking with You?"

The question lingered. She thought back to their early years, how they'd pray together before bed, talk about Scripture on the porch, and dream about the kind of marriage that would honor God. Back then, decisions began with prayer, and gratitude filled their days. Somewhere along the way, that rhythm had been replaced by busyness.

The next morning, she shared her heart with Chris over coffee. He nodded, eyes tired but sincere. "I've felt it too," he admitted. "Like we're still in the same boat, but rowing in different directions."

That night, they didn't try to solve everything. Instead, they sat side by side, opened their Bibles, and quietly invited God back into the center of their marriage. It wasn't dramatic, just simple honesty and a shared desire to start again.

Over the following weeks, they made small but meaningful changes. Morning prayers before the day began. Short devotionals together after the kids went to bed. Decisions made with intentional pauses to ask, "What would honor God here?" Slowly, peace began to replace pressure. The distance between them started to shrink.

Their lives didn't get easier, there were still deadlines, bills, and sleepless nights, but their focus changed. God wasn't just someone they turned to in crisis; He became part of the rhythm of their everyday life.

Lena and Chris discovered that when God moves from the edges to the center, everything else begins to align. Their conversations deepened, their unity strengthened, and their love felt anchored again, not by circumstance, but by the One who held them together.

Because a marriage built with God at the center doesn't just survive — it flourishes, even in the ordinary.

Marriage doesn't drift in a moment — it drifts in inches. But when Christ becomes the center again, everything else falls into place. Peace returns, purpose becomes clearer, and love begins to reflect something far greater than just two people — it begins to echo the heart of God.

Lena and Chris's story is a gentle yet powerful reminder that spiritual drift often happens subtly. It's not usually a dramatic decision to walk away from God, but rather a slow fade, one busy day at a time, one missed prayer at a time, one quiet compromise at a time. Life gets full, responsibilities multiply, and before we know it, the One who was once central becomes peripheral.

Colossians 3:17 brings us back to the heart of what it means to live, and love, in step with Christ: 'And whatever you do, in word or deed, do everything in the name of the Lord Jesus.' That includes marriage. It consists of how we speak to our spouse, how we serve them, how we make decisions together, and even how we handle conflict. When Christ is at the center, everything else begins to align.

Marriage drifts when God becomes an occasional guest rather than a daily guide. But when we realign our hearts and homes around Him, something shifts. Peace begins to return, not because circumstances magically improve, but because our perspective is anchored in truth. Communication deepens because grace becomes the language. Intimacy grows because love is no longer just emotional, it's spiritual. The purpose becomes clearer because we're no longer just building a life together; we're building a testimony.

> God doesn't want to just be a part of your marriage during the emergencies or big decisions. He wants to walk with you in the ordinary. He wants to be there in the quiet mornings, the evening routines, the parenting struggles, and the financial planning. He wants to be the one who shapes your conversations, your priorities, and your affections.

So, if you feel like you and your spouse have drifted, not just from each other, but from God, know this: you don't have to fix everything overnight. You just have to take one step back toward Him. Open the Word together. Pray, even if it feels awkward at first. Invite Him into the everyday moments, not just the milestones.

Because when Christ is the center, your marriage becomes more than a relationship. It becomes a reflection of His love, His grace, and His faithfulness. And that's the kind of love that doesn't just survive the seasons — it thrives through them.

Reflection Question:
What would it look like for God to truly be the center of your marriage?

Couples Challenge:
Pray together before bed every night this week, even if it's just for a minute. Consistency invites God's presence.

Prayer:
Father, forgive us for the times we've tried to lead without You. Take Your rightful place at the center of our marriage and let everything we do bring glory to Your name. Amen.

DAY SEVEN

Prayer of Dedication: "Lord Build Our Home"

Scripture: *Psalm 127:1 (ESV)* — *"Unless the Lord builds the house, those who build it labor in vain."*

Ben and Mariah had just moved into their first home, a cozy, white-sided house with a small front porch, creaky floors, and endless possibilities. It wasn't perfect, but it was theirs. They spent late nights painting walls, unpacking boxes, and dreaming about the life they would build together.

The early days were filled with excitement. They planted flowers in the backyard, hosted friends for Sunday dinners, and made plans for renovations that would one day turn their "starter house" into something picture-perfect. From the outside, it looked like they had everything under control.

But slowly, the strain began to show. The pressure of finances, the weight of daily responsibilities, and the quiet expectations they never voiced began to wear them down. The laughter that once filled the house turned to tense silences and short replies.

One night, after another disagreement about money, Mariah sat on the edge of the bed, tears welling in her eyes. "We've built such a beautiful house," she whispered, "but why doesn't it feel like home?"

When Ben came in and sat beside her, the room fell quiet. For a long moment, neither spoke. Then, almost in unison, they realized what had been missing. They had worked so hard to build a life *for* themselves, but not necessarily *with* the One who had given it to them.

They decided something had to change. From that night on, their focus shifted. They began praying together each morning before work, asking for peace and wisdom in their decisions. They made space to pause before reacting, to listen before speaking, and to invite God into the middle of their plans, not just at the edges.

Over time, their home began to feel different. The arguments didn't vanish, but they softened. The walls no longer just held furniture and décor, they held forgiveness, laughter, and prayer. Their routines became less about control and more about connection.

It wasn't the new furniture, fresh paint, or weekend projects that made the difference. It was a surrender, the decision to let God build what they could not.

In the years that followed, Ben and Mariah often looked around their little house with quiet gratitude. The structure still creaked, the floors still squeaked, but the presence that filled it made it holy ground.

Because when love and faith become the blueprint, a house becomes something greater, a home built not just by human hands, but by the heart of God Himself.

Ben and Mariah's story is a beautiful reminder that a house is not the same as a home. You can fill the walls with photos, the rooms with furniture, and the calendar with routines, but without the Lord at the center, something vital will always feel missing. Psalm 127:1 says, 'Unless the Lord builds the house, those who build it labor in vain.' It's not a warning against hard work, it's an invitation to build with God, not just for Him.

Every couple builds something. We build habits, dreams, traditions, and plans. But the question is: what foundation are we building on? Is it our preferences, our timeline, our vision of success? Or is it rooted in God's wisdom, grace, and presence? When we build without Him, even the most beautiful structures can feel hollow. But when we let Him be the Builder, what we create becomes sacred, full of peace, purpose, and lasting joy.

Ben and Mariah realized that even though they were building together, they weren't building with God. That shift, inviting Him into the center, didn't erase their challenges, but it gave them something stronger to stand on. Their home became more than a place to live; it became a place where grace was practiced, where forgiveness was offered, and where God's presence was welcomed.

Dedication isn't just a moment at the altar or a prayer over a new home, it's a daily choice. Each morning, we decide who is guiding our plans: our own pride or God's presence. When we hand Him the blueprint again and again, He doesn't just bless our home — He builds it into something eternal.

So today, ask yourself: who's building your home? Is it shaped by the pressures of perfection, or by the peace of His presence? Surrender the hammer. Lay down the plans. Let the Lord build something in your marriage that will last beyond the seasons, beyond the struggle, and beyond the surface. That's when a house becomes a haven. That's when your home becomes holy ground.

Reflection Question:
Have you truly invited God to take ownership of your marriage, or are you still the architect?

Couples Challenge:
Hold hands and pray together aloud: "Lord, we give You our marriage. Build what only You can build."

Prayer:
Lord, be the Builder and Keeper of our home. Help us surrender our plans and follow Your design. Let our marriage stand as a testimony of Your faithfulness. Amen.

WEEK TWO

DAYS 8-14

THEME:
COMMUNICATION & CONNECTION:
LEARNING TO HEAR AND BE HEARD

KEY VERSE: JAMES 1:19
Let every person be quick to hear, slow to
speak, slow to anger

Day Eight

The Power of Words

Scripture: *Proverbs 18:21 (ESV) — "Death and life are in the power of the tongue, and those who love it will eat its fruits."*

Eli and Natalie had been married for several years, long enough to settle into routines, rhythms, and patterns, both comforting and familiar. In the early days, their conversations were full of laughter, encouragement, and gentle affirmations. Every word seemed to carry warmth.

But over time, small changes crept in. It wasn't dramatic or overtly hurtful, just sharp, short, and often dismissive.

Eli came home from work exhausted, and Natalie's humor sometimes slipped into sarcasm: "Nice of you to finally join us."

Natalie would share a rough day, and Eli, distracted or tired, would mutter, "Could be worse," barely looking up from his phone.

At first, neither noticed how much these small words chipped away at the atmosphere of their home. The warmth that once wrapped around their days began to fade. Conversations became transactional, frustration hung in the air, and laughter grew scarce.

Then one afternoon, while rummaging through an old drawer, Natalie found a small stack of handwritten notes Eli had left during their first year of marriage. Simple, sincere words that once flowed naturally:

"I believe in you."

"You made a hard day better."

"I'm proud to be your wife."

Tears filled her eyes, not because these truths were gone, but because they had been forgotten, unspoken for far too long.

That night, she placed the notes gently on Eli's side of the bed. When he discovered them, he sat beside her, quiet for a moment, then whispered, "I miss speaking to you like this."

Natalie nodded, her own voice soft, "Me too."

That night, they prayed together, asking God to help them reset not just their hearts, but their words. Slowly, intentionally, they began to speak differently. Not perfectly, but with purpose. They apologized quickly, encouraged often, and chose words that built instead of bruised.

Small phrases became powerful:

"I'm thankful for you."

"That was a kind thing you did."

"I know we're still learning, but I'm committed to you."

Over time, the fog lifted. Their home felt lighter, warmer, and more alive. They realized words were more than communication, they were seeds, capable of nurturing love or sowing division. And when spoken with care, honesty, and grace, they could transform ordinary days into moments of lasting connection.

The story of Eli and Natalie is a powerful reminder that the words we speak in our closest relationships are never neutral. Proverbs 18:21 tells us that the tongue holds the power of life and death. That's not poetic exaggeration — it's spiritual truth. In marriage, every word spoken either builds up or tears down. There is no such thing as a harmless jab when it becomes a pattern. What starts as sarcasm or indifference slowly chips away at intimacy and trust.

James 3:5-6 compares the tongue to a small spark that can set a great forest on fire. Just as a careless word can ignite conflict or resentment, a kind word can spark healing and connection. Eli and Natalie's journey shows that change doesn't begin with grand gestures, but with small, intentional choices. A returned compliment. A heartfelt apology. A quiet prayer for help.

Ephesians 4:29 reminds us, 'Let no corrupting talk come out of your mouths, but only such as is good for building up, as fits the occasion, that it may give grace to those who hear.' This is a call to speak words that strengthen, not weaken. In marriage, that means choosing to affirm rather than accuse, to listen rather than dismiss, and to bless rather than blame.

When we invite God into our speech, we invite Him into our homes. Psalm 141:3 says, 'Set a guard, O Lord, over my mouth; keep watch over the door of my lips!' That's a prayer every couple can adopt. Because when we let God tame our tongues, He begins to soften our hearts. And when our hearts are softened, love has room to breathe again. They didn't need grand speeches — they just needed daily grace-filled words. Because in marriage, speaking life isn't optional — it's sacred. And when God begins to tame our tongues, He starts to heal our homes.

Ultimately, speaking life in marriage is not about being perfect, it's about being purposeful. It's about remembering that your spouse is not your enemy, but your covenant partner. Speak to your spouse as someone made in the image of God, not as your opponent. And every word you speak is either a brick in the foundation or a crack in the wall.

> Words can either breathe life into a marriage or drain it. Every tone, every phrase, every sigh carries weight. God wired language with creative power. He spoke the universe into being. When we speak encouragement, we participate in that same life-giving work; when we lash out, we join in destruction.

Many marriages die not by betrayal, but by a slow erosion of careless speech. Sarcasm replaces sincerity, and silence replaces blessing. But God invites you to speak life again. Simple words like "I'm proud of you," "I forgive you," or "I love you" can heal years of damage.

Let your home be a place where grace is spoken fluently, where forgiveness is freely offered, and where love is not just felt, but heard. Ask God to put a guard over your lips and to fill your words with grace.

Reflection Question:

What tone or habit of speech do you need to surrender to God so your words can bring life instead of harm?

Couples Challenge:

Take turns saying three affirmations about each other today out loud. Let your home echo with life-giving words.

Prayer:

Lord, help us speak with kindness and truth. Let our words be tools of healing, not weapons of hurt. Teach us to speak life into each other daily. Amen.

Day Nine

Listening Like Jesus

Scripture: *Mark 10:51–52 (ESV) — "And Jesus said to him, "What do you want me to do for you?" And the blind man said to him, "Rabbi, let me recover my sight."*

Daniel and Elise had been married nine years, long enough for routines, rhythms, and frustrations to settle into familiar patterns. Lately, though, their conversations felt more like debates than dialogue. Words flew, assumptions piled up, and unspoken resentments grew like clutter they stepped over every day.

One afternoon, after a tense disagreement about parenting, Elise spoke softly, not in anger, but in exhaustion: "You don't really listen to me anymore."

Daniel felt the instinct to defend himself, to list everything he *had* heard, to prove he was paying attention. But something in her tone made him pause. Instead of reacting, he asked quietly, "What do you need from me right now?"

Elise blinked, startled. No one had asked her that recently, not at work, not with the kids, and certainly not during a conflict. Her eyes shimmered with unshed tears. "I need to know that my voice matters to you. That you're really hearing me, not just waiting to be right."

Her words lingered in his mind long after the conversation ended. That evening, Daniel reflected on how he had been listening: not to understand, but to respond, to fix, or to defend. He realized he had been missing the heart behind her words.

He chose to change. He began asking thoughtful questions, giving her space to speak without interruption. He listened not only for the words but for the feelings behind them. He stopped rushing to offer solutions or explanations and focused on being fully present.

The shift wasn't immediate, but over time, Elise noticed. Conversations that once felt like battles started to feel like bridges. Arguments still came, as they always would, but something had changed. There was more empathy, more patience, more connection.

One evening, weeks later, Elise came home after a long day and collapsed on the couch. Daniel sat beside her, not with advice or solutions, but with quiet presence. He took her hand and simply said, "Tell me about your day. I'm listening."

For the first time in months, Elise felt completely heard. And in that moment, Daniel realized that listening like this didn't just resolve conflict — it built intimacy. Their marriage wasn't perfect, but it was growing stronger, not because every problem had disappeared, but because every heart felt noticed.

Because love listens not just to words, but to the person behind them. And when one spouse truly sees the other, even the heaviest burdens feel lighter together.

What Jesus modeled with Bartimaeus is more than a moment of kindness, it is a blueprint for relational healing. Jesus, who already knew the man's need, still asked, 'What do you want me to do for you?' This question created space for dignity, voice, and connection. In marriage, we often assume we know what our spouse needs or feels, but asking, honestly asking, opens the door to deeper understanding.

James 1:19 reminds us, 'Let every person be quick to hear, slow to speak, slow to anger.' This is not just good advice for conflict; it is the posture of love. Being quick to hear means we prioritize understanding over defending. It means we stop rehearsing our next point and start tuning in to what our spouse is really communicating, not just with their words, but with their tone, expression, and silence.

Proverbs 18:2 says, 'A fool takes no pleasure in understanding, but only in expressing his opinion.' In marriage, this kind of self-focused communication can slowly erode trust. But when we choose to listen like Jesus, with patience, humility, and curiosity, we create a safe space for vulnerability to grow.

Daniel and Elise's story show that asking the right question can shift the entire atmosphere of a relationship. When Daniel asked, 'What do you need from me right now?' he wasn't giving up his voice, he was making room for hers. That's what love does. It listens without interrupting. It asks without assuming. It values presence over performance.

Listening is not a weakness — it is a strength under control. It is an act of service, of putting someone else's heart before your own agenda. In Philippians 2:4, Paul writes, 'Let each of you look not only to his own interests, but also to the interests of others.' Listening is one of the most practical ways we live this out in marriage.

> God often speaks through your spouse, too. You might be missing His wisdom because you're too busy forming a reply. Slow down and listen, not just to their words, but to their heart.

If your conversations have become strained or shallow, maybe it's time to stop trying to fix and start trying to hear. Ask the question Jesus asked: 'What do you want me to do for you?' And then, listen, not just with your ears, but with your heart. That's where healing begins.

Reflection Question:
How often do you listen to understand rather than to respond? What needs to change?

Couples Challenge:
Tonight, ask your spouse one open-ended question about how they've been feeling lately and just listen without interrupting.

Prayer:
Jesus, teach us to listen the way You do, with compassion, attention, and patience. Help us hear not only words, but hearts. Amen.

Day Ten

Speaking Truth in Love

Scripture: *Ephesians 4:15 (ESV) — "Rather, speaking the truth in love, we are to grow up in every way into him who is the head, into Christ."*

Joanna and Roger had been married long enough to know each other's weaknesses, and long enough that sometimes, they forgot the importance of gentleness.

One evening, Roger came home late from work, for the third time that week. He stepped through the door with a half-formed apology, only to find Joanna already in the kitchen, arms crossed, frustration written across her face.

"Of course you're late again," she said sharply. "Why even bother telling me anymore?"

The tension ignited instantly. Roger raised his voice in defense. Joanna escalated in response. By the end of the night, the house was quiet, but cold. Their words had conveyed truth, yes, but without care, without love. The honesty had left a wound, not a bridge.

Later, Joanna sat alone on the couch, heart heavy. She knew her words were justified, but the delivery had hurt more than it helped. She realized that truth without love often does more damage than silence.

The next morning, while Roger brewed coffee in the quiet kitchen, Joanna tried again. This time, she paused, took a deep breath, and asked God to guide her words.

"I want you to know how much I miss you," she said softly. "When you're home, you still feel far away. I know work is demanding right now, but I need us. I need you."

Roger set the mug down, surprised by the gentleness in her tone. "I didn't realize how much this was affecting you," he admitted. "I should've paid attention sooner."

That morning sparked a new rhythm of conversation between them, honest, but gentle; straightforward, yet tender. They didn't sweep the issue under the rug; they approached it with humility, grace, and a renewed commitment to understanding one another.

Over time, they learned that truth spoken in love doesn't just convey reality, it nurtures connection, heals misunderstandings, and strengthens the foundation of a marriage.

Honesty paired with care doesn't divide — it unites.

In marriage, it's easy to fall on one side of the scale: truth without tenderness, or love without honesty. But growth happens when both are present. Speaking truth in love doesn't mean avoiding hard conversations, it means choosing timing, words, and tone that reflect Jesus. Not to win a point, but to win a heart.

> Healthy marriages need both truth and tenderness. Truth without love feels harsh; love without truth feels hollow. When we blend both, growth happens. God calls us to communicate in a way that builds up, not beats down.

Speaking truth in love means addressing real issues with gentleness and grace. It means timing matters as much as truth. It means the motive must always be healing, never humiliation. You don't have to shout to be honest; you just have to care more about connection than correction.

Ephesians 4:15 speaks of 'speaking the truth in love.' That's what Joanna had been missing the night before. Truth alone had caused distance. But truth wrapped in love opened the door to healing. It also reminds us that truth and love are not opposing forces — they are partners in spiritual maturity. In marriage, this balance is essential. Without truth, we avoid the real issues and let resentment fester. Without love, we use truth as a weapon rather than a tool for healing. Joanna and Roger's story shows how easy it is to say the right thing in the wrong way, and how damaging that can be.

Proverbs 15:1 says, 'A soft answer turns away wrath, but a harsh word stirs up anger.' The tone we use often determines the outcome of a conversation more than the content. Joanna's first reaction was rooted in frustration, and while her words were technically true, they lacked the softness that invites connection. Her second attempt, however, reflected a heart that desired restoration, not retaliation.

Colossians 4:6 also gives us this wisdom: 'Let your speech always be gracious, seasoned with salt, so that you may know how you ought to answer each person.' Grace-filled truth is the seasoning that makes hard conversations digestible. It doesn't dilute the message, but it makes it easier to receive.

In marriage, we are called not just to speak truth, but to speak it in a way that reflects Christ. That means checking our motives before we speak. Are we trying to heal or to hurt? Are we seeking to understand or to accuse? Are we building a bridge or drawing a line?

Sometimes the most loving thing we can do is speak up. But love changes how we do it. It slows us down. It softens our tone. It reminds us that our spouse is not our enemy, but our teammate. And it helps us remember that the goal of communication is not to win an argument, but to win each other's hearts again and again.

When truth and love walk hand in hand, they lead us toward growth, intimacy, and lasting peace. So, before you speak, pause and pray: 'God, help me say what needs to be said, but help me say it the way You would.'

Reflection Question:

When you need to address something hard, how can you make sure your words build up instead of tear down?

Couples Challenge:

If something's been on your heart, talk about it today, but begin and end the conversation with affirmation and prayer.

Prayer:

Lord, help us to balance honesty with humility. Let our conversations be filled with both grace and truth so we can grow together in You. Amen.

Day Eleven

Breaking the Silence Walls

Scripture: *Proverbs 15:1 (ESV) — "A soft answer turns away wrath, but a harsh word stirs up anger."*

Anna and Marcus lived in a quiet house, but it was the kind of quiet that pressed down on them rather than comforted them. In the weeks following a painful disagreement, their conversations had dwindled to the practical necessities, dishes washed, appointments remembered, but their hearts seemed to drift further apart.

Marcus told himself he was keeping the peace by holding back, giving both of them space to cool down. Anna, on the other hand, felt the silence as something heavier: distance, maybe even indifference. Each passing day added weight to the walls growing between them, until even sharing the same room felt like crossing a chasm.

One evening, they found themselves on opposite ends of the couch. The TV flickered with background noise, but neither was really watching. Anna's voice, soft and tentative, finally cut through the quiet. "Do you... still care the way you used to?"

Marcus turned toward her, startled by the vulnerability in her question. For a moment, he considered answering defensively, but something inside him urged a gentler approach. He inhaled slowly and met her gaze. "I never stopped caring," he said, his voice quiet but steady. "I just didn't know how to fix what felt broken without making it worse."

Tears gathered in Anna's eyes. She nodded, her voice barely more than a whisper. "Me too."

The silence between them had been broken, not with argument, blame, or pride, but with honesty and tenderness. That night, they stayed up talking, exploring the hurt, acknowledging the longing, and sharing what they still hoped for. Their words didn't build walls; they built a bridge back to each other, one careful, heartfelt step at a time.

Proverbs 15:1 says, 'A soft answer turns away wrath.' In their case, it also turned away distance. One soft word became the spark that melted weeks of tension.

This reminds us that the way we respond matters just as much as what we say. A soft answer doesn't mean a weak one, it means a wise and Spirit-led one. In moments of tension, our natural instinct may be to defend, withdraw, or retaliate. But gentleness has a surprising strength. It doesn't ignore pain, but it chooses humility over hostility.

In Anna and Marcus's story, we see that silence isn't always peace. Sometimes, it's just a quiet form of conflict. When we avoid hard conversations, we may think we're keeping things calm, but we're actually allowing distance to grow. Ephesians 4:26 says, 'Do not let the sun go down on your anger.' That doesn't mean every issue must be solved in a day, but it does mean we shouldn't let unresolved hurt turn into prolonged disconnection.

Gentleness is not passivity — it's intentional kindness. Galatians 5:22 tells us that gentleness is a fruit of the Spirit, meaning it's a sign of God's work in our hearts. When we respond to our spouse with softness, even when we're hurting, we reflect the character of Christ. Jesus never avoided truth, but He always delivered it with compassion. Choosing gentleness doesn't mean avoiding truth, it means honoring your spouse's heart even when it hurts.

> One gentle phrase can do what hours of silence never will, it can open a door. Marcus's quiet but honest response didn't erase the pain, but it invited Anna back into connection. That's the power of a soft answer. It doesn't just turn away wrath — it turns hearts toward each other.

If you're waiting for the perfect moment to fix things, remember healing rarely begins with a perfect moment. It starts with a humble one. Don't underestimate the power of a whisper of grace. Sometimes, the smallest words, spoken with love, can begin the most significant breakthroughs. The goal isn't to avoid conflict — it's to approach it with gentleness.

Reflection Question:

What's one topic or hurt you've been avoiding that needs gentle, honest conversation?

Couples Challenge:

Have a "grace conversation" tonight. Choose one lingering issue and talk about it kindly, seeking understanding, not blame.

Prayer:

Father, help us to speak softly and wisely. Please give us the courage to face hard things with gentleness and teach us to rebuild connections where silence has settled. Amen.

Day Twelve

Fighting Fair, Loving Deep

Scripture: *Ephesians 4:26–27 (ESV) — "Be angry and do not sin; do not let the sun go down on your anger, and give no opportunity to the devil."*

Matt and Lily were a couple who lived life with intensity, not just in love, but in everything they did. Parenting, ministry, careers, they approached each challenge with passion. But that same passion sometimes ignited their disagreements, turning ordinary conversations into heated battles.

One Thursday evening, a discussion about finances escalated quickly. Words were exchanged that cut deeper than either one intended. By the time they went to bed, silence had settled over the house like a heavy fog. Faces turned away, hearts hardened, and the warmth of their connection felt distant.

Both knew that letting the day end in anger would only allow resentment to grow. But the easier choice seemed to be retreating into quiet, ignoring the tension until morning.

Then Lily's voice broke the stillness, soft and hesitant. "I hate that we're ending the day like this," she whispered.

Matt exhaled slowly, turning toward her. "Me too," he admitted. "I let my anger speak louder than my love."

What followed wasn't an argument, but a conversation grounded in humility and understanding. They spoke carefully, listening as much as they shared. They paused, prayed together, and leaned in instead of shutting each other out.

That night, they discovered an important truth: conflict didn't have to fracture their relationship. When handled with patience, honesty, and grace, even the hardest disagreements could strengthen trust and deepen love. Their connection was not about being right, it was about staying close, even in the midst of conflict.

Conflict is inevitable, but chaos is optional.

Every couple, no matter how strong their bond, will face moments of tension. It's not the presence of conflict that determines the health of a relationship, but how it's handled. Scripture doesn't tell us to suppress our anger — it tells us to steward it well. Ephesians 4:26–27 reminds us, 'Be angry and do not sin; do not let the sun go down on your anger and give no opportunity to the devil.' This verse acknowledges that anger is a real emotion, but it also warns us of its dangers when left unchecked.

Matt and Lily's story is a powerful reminder that unresolved anger becomes fertile ground for division. When we allow the sun to set on our bitterness, even for one night, we give the enemy a foothold. The longer anger lingers, the more it festers, and the harder it becomes to extend grace. But when we choose humility over pride, connection over control, something beautiful happens — healing begins.

Fighting fair means we are not trying to win the argument but win each other's hearts. It means we pause to listen, pray for wisdom, and pursue peace. We don't attack our spouse — we attack the issue. We speak truth, but we do it wrapped in grace. We don't use our words as weapons or bring up past failures to score points. Instead, we respond with gentleness, seeking to understand before being understood.

> Couples who fight fair learn to pause, pray, and approach. They refuse to weaponize words or reopen old wounds. When handled with grace, disagreements can actually strengthen trust. The devil looks for cracks in communication; don't give him space.

God designed marriage to be a place of safety and unity, not strife and division. When couples adopt the principle of resolving anger before the day ends, they build a habit of emotional honesty and spiritual maturity. Even in disagreement, they can grow closer, because their goal isn't to dominate, it's to deepen trust.

The enemy thrives in silence, resentment, and unresolved tension. But when couples choose to lean in, even through tears and frustration, they shut the door on his schemes. Conflict may be inevitable, but chaos is optional. And when handled with grace and truth, even the most challenging conversations can become steppingstones toward greater intimacy and trust.

Reflection Question:

When conflict arises, what habits or reactions make peace more complicated to find, and how can you change them?

Couples Challenge:

Create a "fight fair" rule together, something like, "We won't raise our voices" or "We'll pray before bed no matter what."

Prayer:

Lord, teach us to disagree without disrespect. Help us handle conflict with wisdom and keep our hearts soft toward each other and You. Amen.

Day Thirteen

Rebuilding Emotional Safety

Scripture: *Colossians 3:8–10 (ESV) — "...and have put on the new self, which is being renewed in knowledge after the image of its creator."*

Josh and Alyssa were opposites in more ways than one. He liked to talk things out immediately; she needed space to process. He used humor to lighten tension; she needed empathy before laughter. Over time, these differences began to feel like personal offenses instead of personality traits.

One day, they had a minor disagreement about something trivial, a missed text, a forgotten errand, but it quickly escalated. Josh, feeling stressed from work, snapped with a sarcastic comment: 'Well, I guess I can't do anything right, can I?'

Alyssa's face fell. The moment grew quiet, and she walked out of the room without a word. Josh thought she was overreacting, but deep down, he knew that wasn't the only time his words had left a dent.

Later that night, he found her sitting on the back porch. She didn't look angry, she looked tired. Tired of feeling misunderstood. Tired of feeling unsafe to show weakness.

Josh sat down beside her and gently said, 'I've realized I've been quick to speak and slow to listen. I've let my reactions push you away when I should have been protecting your heart.'

Alyssa looked at him with tears in her eyes and said, 'I want to feel like this is a safe space again. Like it's okay to be upset without being shut down.'

Josh nodded slowly. That night, something shifted in him. He began to see emotional safety not as something she had to earn by being less emotional, but as something he was responsible for creating and protecting with his words, tone, and attitude.

From then on, they made small, intentional changes, slowing down before speaking, asking thoughtful questions instead of jumping to conclusions, trading sarcasm for sincerity. It wasn't always smooth. It took time. But they kept choosing each other over being right and understanding over assumption.

Slowly, trust began to rebuild. The same porch that once held silence now echoed with grace. Love grows best in an atmosphere of kindness, where both people feel safe to be seen, not just for their strengths, but also in their struggles, and still be held with care.

Emotional safety is the soil where love grows. Without it, communication dries up. Safety doesn't mean perfection, it means knowing your heart is safe in the other person's care. When your spouse feels judged, dismissed, or unheard, they begin to retreat.

Colossians 3:8–10 calls us to put off the old self and put on the new, a self that is being renewed in the image of our Creator. This transformation impacts every area of our lives, especially our relationships. In marriage, the old self often shows up as defensiveness, sarcasm, impatience, or miscommunication. But the new self, shaped by Christ, responds with gentleness, understanding, and grace.

Josh and Alyssa's story remind us that emotional safety isn't automatic. It's something we build, protect, and sometimes rebuild. When a spouse feels emotionally unsafe, they begin to shut down, not because they don't care, but because they're trying to protect their heart from further harm. This is why our words, tone, and timing matter so deeply. The way we respond in moments of tension can either build a bridge or erect a wall.

> Emotional safety doesn't mean you'll never disagree or get frustrated. It means that even in those moments, your spouse knows they won't be belittled, dismissed, or ignored. It means they can bring their whole selves, mess and all, and still be met with love.

This kind of safety is cultivated through intentional choices: choosing to listen rather than react, to ask questions rather than make assumptions, and to affirm rather than accuse. When we trade sarcasm for sincerity and criticism for compassion, we reflect the heart of Christ in our relationships.

God's grace is the atmosphere in which emotional healing takes place. Just as He meets us with kindness and patience, we are called to extend that same spirit to each other. Your marriage becomes a safe space when your spouse knows they can bring their fears, failures, and feelings, and instead of being pushed away, they'll be embraced.

Trust may take time to rebuild, but it's never out of reach when both hearts are willing. It starts by choosing gentleness over sarcasm, curiosity over criticism, and patience over pressure. When you protect each other's vulnerability, intimacy deepens. As you put on the new self-daily, let your home be a place where love grows deep because safety runs wide. Let your actions say, 'You are safe with me, even when it's hard, even when we're hurting, even when we're growing.' That's the kind of love that reflects Christ and renews the heart.

Reflection Question:

What actions or words from you help your spouse feel most emotionally safe and which ones might do the opposite?

Couples Challenge:

Ask your spouse, "What makes you feel safe when we talk?" Then practice one of those things this week.

Prayer:

Jesus, fill our hearts with gentleness. Help us create an atmosphere where honesty feels safe and grace flows freely. Amen.

Day Fourteen

Unity in Prayer and Purpose

Scripture: *Matthew 18:19–20 (ESV) — "Again I say to you, if two of you agree on earth about anything they ask, it will be done for them by my Father in heaven."*

Liam and Teresa were exhausted. Between their new baby, long work hours, and the weight of trying to keep up with everything, their marriage felt more like a team of task managers than a union of hearts. They weren't fighting, exactly, but the deep connection they once had felt like it was slipping through the cracks.

They both loved God and attended church, but their faith had become individual routines rather than something they shared. They prayed on their own, but never together. Somehow it had always felt awkward, maybe too vulnerable, too intimate, even a bit unnecessary.

One night after a particularly draining day, tensions were high. Teresa had cried over a sink full of dishes, and Liam had escaped into his laptop, and neither had said much all evening.

As they got ready for bed in tired silence, Liam hesitated, then turned to her.

'Can we just pray?' he asked.

Teresa looked surprised, then nodded, maybe more out of desperation than anything else. They sat on the edge of the bed, hands clutching tightly, and Liam, in soft, stumbling words, prayed:

'God, we're tired. We don't know how to feel close to each other right now. But we want You in the middle of this. Help us figure this out.'

Teresa added, 'Help us stay connected when it's hard even to talk.'

The prayer was under a minute. But something shifted.

They both cried, not from sadness, but from the strange relief of finally handing their mess to the One who could hold it. The walls between them started to soften. It wasn't a dramatic overnight fix, but praying together realigned them not just with each other, but with the God who brought them together in the first place.

When Jesus said, 'If two of you agree on earth about anything they ask, it will be done for them by my Father in heaven,' He wasn't just giving a promise about answered prayer, He was revealing the power of spiritual unity. For married couples, this unity is especially sacred. It's not just about agreeing on decisions or sharing responsibilities; it's about inviting God into the very center of your relationship.

Liam and Teresa's story show how easy it is for couples to drift into parallel lives, especially when life gets overwhelming. They weren't fighting, they were just disconnected. And sometimes, that quiet distance can be more dangerous than loud arguments. But when they chose to pray together, even in their exhaustion and awkwardness, something shifted. Not everything was fixed in a moment, but their hearts began to realign, first with God, then with each other.

Prayer between spouses is powerful not because of the words spoken, but because of the posture it creates. It humbles pride, quiets assumptions, and reminds both hearts that they're on the same team. When you pray together, you're not just talking to God, you're reminding each other that He is your shared foundation, your common anchor.

This kind of spiritual agreement builds a deeper intimacy than words or affection alone. It creates a rhythm where God is not just part of Sunday mornings, but part of your everyday connection. And it doesn't have to be long or eloquent. A whispered prayer before the day begins or a simple 'God, help us' at night can change the atmosphere of your home.

Couples who pray together regularly often find that misunderstandings decrease and empathy increases. It's hard to stay bitter toward someone you've just invited God to bless. Prayer becomes a bridge, especially when emotions run high or words fall short.

Let prayer become more than a last resort or an emergency response; make it a daily rhythm. When you agree together in prayer, you're not just asking God to move, you're aligning yourselves with His heart and with each other. That's where true unity begins, and where love finds its deepest roots. Even thirty seconds together can shift an atmosphere.

Reflection Question:
How consistent are you in praying together, and what gets in the way of making it a priority?

Couples Challenge:
Commit to praying together every day this week, even a short prayer before bed or before work.

Prayer:
Father, thank You for the gift of prayer. Unite our hearts as we seek You together. Teach us to agree in faith and walk in purpose as one. Amen.

WEEK THREE

DAYS 15-21

THEME:

LOVE IN ACTION: CHOOSING SACRIFICE OVER SELF

KEY VERSE: PHILIPPIANS 2:3-4

Do nothing from selfish ambition or conceit, but in humility count others more significant than yourselves

Day Fifteen

Love That Lowers Self

Scripture: *John 13:14–15 (ESV) — "If I then, your Lord and Teacher, have washed your feet, you also ought to wash one another's feet."*

It was their fifth anniversary, and Shelly had quietly hoped for flowers or maybe dinner at their favorite little Italian restaurant. But when she walked into the kitchen after a long, exhausting day, she was greeted instead by the soft hum of the dishwasher, the clean scent of lemon, and the sight of Tony, with rolled-up sleeves and sudsy hands, scrubbing the inside of the oven for the first time in years.

A little surprised, Shelly blinked. 'What are you doing?' she asked.

Tony looked over his shoulder, a little sheepish. 'I know you've been running on empty these days. I thought I'd handle a few things you usually do. It's not fancy, I just didn't want you walking into more work.'

Shelly felt a lump form in her throat. Not because it was grand, but because it wasn't. It was quiet. Thoughtful. Real.

In that moment, what struck her was the way love can show up, not in dramatic gestures, but in the mundane, unseen acts. This wasn't about impressing anyone. It was about care. Intentional, ordinary, beautiful care.

Later that evening, as they sat side by side on the porch, hands intertwined, Shelly whispered, 'That meant more than flowers.'

Tony smiled softly. 'I figured sometimes love needs soap instead of roses.'

In a world that often celebrates performance and recognition, Tony had chosen simplicity. He had placed humility above attention. And in that, Shelly felt deeply seen.

Over time, it became their quiet rhythm, to love each other in the unnoticed ways. A coffee cup set out early, a gas tank filled before the warning light came on, a pause during stress instead of a sharp response, a warm blanket tossed over the other during a late evening nap.

They learned that when love is expressed through service, it doesn't lower either of them. It lifts them both.

John 13:14–15 gives us a powerful picture of love in action: Jesus, the Son of God, kneeling to wash the feet of His disciples. Jesus didn't just talk about love; He demonstrated it with a towel and a basin. The Son of God, on His knees, washing the dirt off His disciples' feet. And then He told us to do the same. In the context of marriage, this kind of love isn't always about grand gestures or romantic surprises. Often, it's about the quiet, unseen acts of service that speak louder than words.

In a world that prizes recognition, Jesus modeled humility. True love lowers itself. It notices needs without being asked. It chooses service over status, surrender over spotlight. In marriage, that might look like doing the unseen chores, offering a gentle word when you'd rather correct, or letting your spouse's needs come first.

When both partners live this way, no one feels small, both feel cherished.

Tony's decision to clean the kitchen rather than buy flowers may have seemed simple. Still, it reflected something profound: a heart tuned to his wife's weariness, a willingness to serve without being asked, and a love that values action over applause. That's the kind of love Jesus modeled, a love that bends low, not because it has to, but because it wants to.

In marriage, serving one another doesn't diminish your value; it elevates your connection. It says, 'I see you. I care about what matters to you. I'm willing to lay down my comfort for your good.' And when both spouses adopt this posture, the home's atmosphere changes. Resentment fades. Gratitude grows. Intimacy deepens.

> True love doesn't wait to be noticed. It notices. It anticipates needs, not for recognition, but out of genuine care. It chooses the towel over the spotlight. And in that posture of humility, both hearts are lifted.

Whether it's folding laundry, preparing coffee, or offering a kind word when irritation would be easier, these small acts of service become sacred. They reflect the heart of Christ and build a foundation of trust and tenderness. Love like this doesn't just survive the everyday — it thrives in it.

So, ask yourself today: where can I pick up the towel in my marriage? Not because I have to, but because I get to. Because when love leads through service, both hearts are refreshed.

Reflection Question:
Where might pride be keeping you from serving your spouse joyfully?

Couples Challenge:
Do one humble act of service for your spouse today, something practical that speaks love without words.

Prayer:
Lord Jesus, teach us to love like You, on our knees, with open hands. Please help us serve one another with joy and humility. Amen.

Day Sixteen

The Gift of Everyday Sacrifice

Scripture: *Romans 12:1 (ESV) — "Present your bodies as a living sacrifice, holy and acceptable to God, which is your spiritual worship."*

It had been one of those weeks, deadlines piling up, kids running on minimal sleep, and the coffee pot breaking down on Monday like the universe was playing a joke. By Friday evening, Sarah was craving one thing: quiet. She had just curled up with a book when she heard the attic ladder creak and her husband's footsteps overhead.

'He's finally fixing that box of Christmas lights,' she thought.

Ten minutes later, her phone buzzed. It was a message from Eric:

'Hey, can you help me really quick? I can't find the labeled box.'

She sighed before she could stop herself. She had asked him to sort the attic weeks ago. She was tired. She was cozy. The last thing she wanted to do was dig through dusty boxes in old sneakers.

But something shifted in her. She realized that love doesn't always show up as romance or effort-free affection. Sometimes, it shows up inconveniently, asking for your time, your energy, your presence, just when you're low on all three.

So, she got up. She tied her hair, slipped on her shoes, and climbed the ladder.

In that cramped attic with a single dim bulb and the smell of old pine decorations, they found more than a box of lights. They found laughter as they scrolled through forgotten ornaments and old holiday photos. They shared memories. They shared space. They remembered how much joy they had built together.

It wasn't really about the lights. It was about what happens when one person sets aside comfort to meet the other where they are.

Eric never knew what Sarah gave up in that moment, her quiet, her comfort, her exasperation. But the impact was felt. Their connection deepened not through grand gestures but through small acts of selflessness that slowly built trust.

Their marriage was made stronger each time one of them chose to show up, especially when it was inconvenient. Real love, they discovered, thrives in those hidden moments, not in perfection, but in presence.

Sometimes the most meaningful offerings in a relationship happen in the attic, when you choose togetherness over ease, and the ordinary becomes sacred.

Sacrifice doesn't always look dramatic, it often looks like patience, restraint, or showing up when it's inconvenient. God calls us to be *living* sacrifices, meaning we lay ourselves down daily, not just once.

Romans 12:1 calls us to present our bodies as a living sacrifice, holy and acceptable to God. This isn't a one-time act; it's a daily posture. It means offering up our time, energy, preferences, and even our comfort in response to God's love. And often, the most sacred sacrifices don't happen on a stage but in the quiet corners of everyday life, like an attic on a Friday night.

Sarah's story reminds us that love doesn't always arrive with fireworks or fanfare. Sometimes it shows up in the form of tired feet climbing a ladder, or a willing heart choosing presence over personal comfort. These moments may seem small, but in God's eyes, they are deeply significant. Why? Because they reflect His own heart, a love that gives, even when it's costly.

In marriage, sacrifice often looks like surrendering the desire always to be right. It looks like offering grace when you feel like snapping or showing up when you'd rather shut down. These aren't dramatic gestures, but they are holy ones. When we choose unity over pride and connection over convenience, we're not just loving our spouse, we're worshiping God.

This kind of love doesn't always get noticed. Your spouse may never fully understand the cost of a quiet sacrifice. But God sees. He sees every time you hold your tongue, every time you choose to serve, every time you put your spouse's needs ahead of your own. And He uses those moments to build something lasting, something eternal.

So please don't underestimate the power of showing up when it's inconvenient. Those are the moments that shape a marriage, that deepen trust, and that reflect the heart of Christ. Real love often grows in the unseen places, through small acts of selflessness that become sacred offerings to God.

Your spouse may never see every effort you make, but God does. And He uses each quiet surrender to build something eternal.

Reflection Question:
What's one "small sacrifice" you could offer today that would bless your spouse and honor God?

Couples Challenge:
Each of you pick one act of quiet sacrifice to do for the other today and don't announce it. Let love speak through action.

Prayer:
Father, help us see every sacrifice as worship. Use our daily choices to shape us into the likeness of Christ. Amen.

DAY SEVENTEEN

When it's Hard to Give Grace

Scripture: *Colossians 3:13 (ESV) — "Bearing with one another and, if one has a complaint against another, forgiving each other; as the Lord has forgiven you, so you also must forgive."*

Cindy stood at the kitchen sink, staring blankly at the half-washed dishes. Cold water ran over her fingers, but her hands hadn't moved in minutes. The sound of the front door clicking shut echoed through the silence, and she knew Alex was home.

It had been three days since the argument. It started small, something about the budget, but had escalated into sharp words and silent glares. Since then, they had danced around each other like polite strangers. And now, Cindy carried the weight of his words like invisible luggage, dragging behind her with every step.

She had been waiting, waiting for him to say sorry first, to make it right, to see how deeply he had hurt her. But as she stood there, unmoving, the real question nudged her heart: Was she willing to let go even if he didn't say everything she needed to hear?

Forgiveness was never easy. It wasn't saying what he did didn't hurt. It wasn't pretending everything was fine. It was choosing to love through the wound. To release the desire to win or to even the score. She thought of all the times Jesus had gently released her from her own guilt, from her own sharp words and stubborn silences. Grace had been given when she least deserved it.

So, she turned off the water, dried her hands, and walked toward the living room. Alex looked up, surprised as she sat beside him.

'I don't want us stuck here,' she said softly. 'I was hurt. But I love you more than I want to be right.'

Alex's eyes filled. He reached for her hand.

Forgiveness opened the door. It broke the chain. And in that quiet act of grace, love exhaled again.

Marriage isn't a courtroom. It's a covenant where two souls learn, day by day, that grace is not weakness, but the strength that holds them together.

Forgiveness is love's hardest expression, and its most powerful. Grace costs something. But marriage without grace becomes a courtroom, not a covenant.

Colossians 3:13 calls us to bear with one another and forgive, just as the Lord has forgiven us. That's a high calling, especially in marriage, where the wounds can feel personal and deep. But it's also one of the most powerful ways love proves itself. Forgiveness is not weakness; it is strength in its most Christlike form.

Cindy's story reminds us that forgiveness often begins before the apology ever comes. It's not about pretending the hurt didn't happen or brushing pain under the rug. It's about choosing to release the offense, not because the other person has perfectly repented, but because we know what it's like to be forgiven ourselves. Jesus didn't wait for us to get everything right before He offered grace. And in marriage, we're called to reflect that same heart.

> When we withhold forgiveness, we may feel like we're protecting ourselves, but in reality, we're chaining our hearts to the very pain we want to escape. Bitterness builds walls, but grace builds bridges. Forgiveness doesn't erase the past, but it opens the door to healing. It says, 'I love you more than I need to be right. I choose us over resentment.'

Marriage isn't a courtroom where we tally offenses and wait for justice. It's a covenant where we learn to extend mercy, just as we've received it. And while grace costs something, our pride, our right to retaliate, it also gives something far greater: freedom, connection, and peace.

Forgiveness is love in motion. It's what keeps a marriage breathing when conflict tries to suffocate it. So, when you're hurt, don't wait for the perfect apology to let go. Take your pain to Jesus, let Him carry it, and choose to forgive, not because your spouse always deserves it, but because grace is how love survives, heals, and grows.

Reflection Question:

Is there a wound you're still carrying that needs the release of forgiveness?

Couples Challenge:

Share with your spouse one area where you need to extend or receive grace and pray for each other.

Prayer:

Jesus, teach us to forgive as You forgave us, fully, freely, and forever. Heal what's broken and fill our hearts with Your grace. Amen.

DAY EIGHTEEN

Serving with Joy, Not Duty

Scripture: *Galatians 5:13 (ESV) — "Through love serve one another."*

It had been one of those long Tuesdays, the kind where everything felt like an effort. Laundry was piled high, the kids had left a trail of toys in every room, and Emma still hadn't had a moment to herself. By the time her husband, Jared, walked through the door, she was already two steps into exhaustion and frustration.

'Hey, hon,' he said, trying to smile, loosening his tie. 'Tough day?'

Instead of answering, Emma nodded and turned back to the kitchen, where the last of the dishes waited. She could almost hear her thoughts grumbling: again, another dinner made, another mess cleaned, another evening where she'd give and give... and maybe no one would even notice.

As she scrubbed a pan, a quiet whisper surfaced in her heart, not audible, but unmistakable: Who are you really doing this for?

She paused.

The answer unsettled her. Lately, she had been serving out of habit, maybe even duty. The joy had slowly leaked out, replaced by a silent tally of who had done more.

But what if this messy kitchen was a mission field? What if folding socks and listening closely at the dinner table were a way to reflect God's heart, not just to her family, but to the One who saw every small act?

That night, Emma reset her perspective. She didn't force a fake smile or pretend the work was easy. But she chose joy. Not because the tasks were lighter, but because she remembered why she was doing them.

When Jared thanked her for dinner, she simply smiled and said, 'You're welcome,' not needing praise to validate her. She had already offered it as worship.

Love in marriage isn't proven in grand gestures — it's shown in the quiet willingness to serve when no one's clapping. And when it's done with joy, even the smallest act becomes a sacred echo of God's love.

Service without joy becomes resentment; service with joy becomes worship. God calls us to serve one another not out of obligation, but out of love.

Galatians 5:13 reminds us that freedom in Christ isn't a license for self-indulgence, it's an invitation to love through service. In marriage, that kind of love is rarely flashy. It's found in the unnoticed, repetitive, behind-the-scenes acts that keep a home running and a relationship thriving.

Emma's story is familiar to many. The weight of daily responsibilities can easily turn service into drudgery. Over time, what began as love can quietly shift into obligation. And when we start keeping score, who did more, who noticed less, we lose sight of the deeper purpose behind our service.

But God sees what others might miss. He sees the late-night laundry, the quiet prayers whispered over a sleeping spouse, the decision to listen with patience instead of reacting in frustration. When we serve our spouse with love, even when it's hard, we're not just helping them, we're honoring God.

Service becomes sacred when it's offered with joy, not because the task is enjoyable, but because we remember who we're ultimately serving. Colossians 3:23 says, 'Whatever you do, work heartily, as for the Lord and not for men.' That includes the unseen acts of love in marriage.

> When your effort feels invisible, know that God sees every sacrifice. He notices every small act done in love. And when you serve with a heart aligned to Him, even the most ordinary things become holy.

When serving your spouse feels hard, remember, you're ultimately serving Christ. Every meal cooked, every prayer whispered, every patient conversation becomes sacred when offered to Him. Joy is found not in being noticed, but in knowing you're reflecting God's heart.

So don't wait for applause. Don't serve just to be appreciated. Let your love speak in the quiet moments, because that's where God often does His deepest work. And in those moments, joy isn't found in recognition, but in knowing you're reflecting the servant heart of Christ.

Reflection Question:

What helps you keep your service motivated by love rather than by guilt or routine?

Couples Challenge:

Each time you serve your spouse today, whisper a quick prayer of gratitude instead of expecting thanks.

Prayer:

Lord, renew our joy in serving one another. Let every act of love we give become a reflection of Your goodness and grace. Amen.

Day Nineteen

Carry Each Other's Burdens

Scripture: *Galatians 6:2 (ESV) — "Bear one another's burdens, and so fulfill the law of Christ."*

It was 6:00 a.m. when Nathan woke to the sound of the shower running and saw the soft light under the bathroom door. Emily was already up, again. He knew she'd been burning the candle at both ends lately, trying to balance work deadlines, school emails for the kids, and the endless to-do list of a home that never seemed to rest.

Nathan stretched, sat at the edge of the bed, and paused. If he were honest, he had been coasting a bit. Leaving her to carry more than her share because he was tired too. But that morning, something stirred in him that went deeper than guilt, it was love. Love that didn't calculate who had done more yesterday, but simply said, 'I see your burden... let me shoulder it with you.'

Without saying a word, he headed to the kitchen, started the coffee, and packed the kids' lunches, the small things Emily always did, unseen. When she came out later with damp hair and tired eyes, she stopped at the counter, surprised.

'You didn't have to do this,' she said quietly.

'I know,' he replied, placing a thermos in her hand. 'But I wanted to walk beside you today, not behind you.'

That day didn't erase her stress or fix everything instantly. But it reminded her that she wasn't alone. That someone saw the weight she carried and chose to lean underneath it with her.

Marriage isn't always clean lines and equal shares. Some days are uneven and heavy. But love shows up, not to fix the struggle, but to share it. To say, 'Your burden is my burden. Together, we'll get through this.'

And in that holy give-and-take, hearts are knit closer, and the everyday loads we carry become a powerful reflection of the love Christ first gave us.

Galatians 6:2 calls us to bear one another's burdens, and in doing so, we fulfill the law of Christ, the law of love. In marriage, this isn't just a nice idea; it's a daily calling. Life doesn't always hand out equal portions of stress, energy, or emotional capacity. Some days, one spouse is stretched thin while the other has a little more to give. And that's where love steps in, not to fix everything, but to help carry the weight.

Nathan's quiet gesture that morning wasn't about grand heroics. It was about presence. About seeing his wife's exhaustion and choosing to come alongside her. That's the kind of love that reflects Christ, love that notices, responds, and sacrifices, even in small ways.

> Marriage isn't about keeping score or dividing duties down the middle 50/50. It's about carrying 100% together. Some days, one of you will carry more simply because the other can't. And that's not failure — that's faithfulness. It's choosing to say, 'I'm here. I see you. Let me help.'

Bearing one another's burdens might look like doing the dishes without being asked, praying when your spouse is too tired to speak, or just sitting quietly and listening when they need to unload. It's not about having all the answers, it's about refusing to let them carry the weight alone.

When we carry each other's everyday burdens, we mirror the heart of Jesus, who carried our most significant burden to the cross. And in those small, sacred moments of shared struggle, love deepens. Trust grows. And the bond between two hearts becomes stronger than the weight of any to-do list or weary morning.

So, when the day feels uneven, don't pull away, lean in. Let your love be a shoulder, a helping hand, a quiet strength. Christ carried our most significant burden on the cross; we honor Him when we shoulder each other's everyday loads. Because in marriage, the goal isn't perfect balance, it's faithful presence. And that's where Christ is most clearly seen.

Reflection Question:

What burden is your spouse carrying right now, and how can you lighten it this week?

Couples Challenge:

Ask your spouse, "What can I do to make your week easier?" and follow through.

Prayer:

Jesus, teach us to carry each other's burdens with grace. Make our marriage a picture of Your compassionate love. Amen.

DAY TWENTY

The Strength of Gentle Love

Scripture: *1 Peter 3:4 (ESV) — "Let your adorning be the hidden person of the heart with the imperishable beauty of a gentle and quiet spirit, which in God's sight is very precious."*

Leah could feel the tension the moment her husband, David, walked through the door. His shoulders were tight, his words clipped, and that frustrated look in his eyes was all too familiar. He had clearly had a hard day.

Dinner was already on the table, the kids were noisy, and she had her own stress simmering just beneath the surface. As he dropped his bag with a thud and muttered something about work being a mess, Leah felt her own frustration rise.

She wanted to snap back, to match his tone with one of her own. She thought, 'I've been juggling everything here while you're off stewing in your bad mood. Why should I be patient when he's not even trying?'

But in that split second, something softened in her.

She looked at him, not as the man who had just ignored her hello, but as the man who was weary, burdened, and maybe just a little lost in the mess of the day. Instead of setting the mood with sharp words, she took a breath and replied gently, 'Rough day? Want to talk about it after dinner?'

David paused. The edge in his posture eased. He looked up, surprised, like her kindness had caught him off guard and touched something deeper than irritation.

'Yeah,' he said, his voice lower, 'Sorry I came in like that. I shouldn't have dumped it all here.'

That night, they sat on the porch after the kids went to bed. He shared. She listened. No defenses, no blame. Just calmness and connection.

Leah learned that day that gentleness wasn't shrinking back, it was stepping forward with strength under control. It created a safe space, invited honesty, and built trust.

Marriage isn't kept strong by who gets the last word or who proves the point. It's strengthened when one person chooses to respond gently, even when their feelings scream otherwise.

1 Peter 3:4 reminds us that God values the hidden person of the heart, the part of us that isn't loud or flashy, but steady and gentle. In a world that often rewards the loudest voice or the sharpest comeback, Scripture calls us to something far richer: a spirit that is quiet, calm, and deeply anchored in grace. In marriage, this kind of spirit is not only precious to God, but also powerful in practice.

Leah's story shows us that gentleness doesn't mean passivity. It's not about ignoring your own emotions or pretending everything is fine. Gentleness is strength under control. It's choosing to respond with grace when your feelings are pulling you toward frustration. It's seeing your spouse not as an opponent to be corrected, but as a partner to be understood.

When Leah chose a gentle response, she didn't lose her voice — she used it to create peace. That one soft question, offered instead of a sharp reply, shifted the entire atmosphere of their evening. It opened the door for honesty and connection. That's the beauty of a gentle spirit — it diffuses tension and invites healing.

In marriage, the goal isn't to win the argument or prove the point. It's to protect the connection. Gentleness builds trust. It tells your spouse, 'You are safe with me, even when things are hard.' It doesn't mean you never express hurt or frustration, but it means you do so in a way that preserves dignity and invites reconciliation.

Choosing gentleness doesn't come naturally in heated moments. It's a fruit of the Spirit, something we grow into as we walk closely with Christ. But when we choose it, especially when it's hard, we make space for the Holy Spirit to work in us and between us.

So, the next time tension rises, pause. Breathe. Ask God to help you respond with the kind of strength that doesn't shout but gently steadies. Because in a marriage rooted in gentleness, love isn't just heard, it's felt, and it's trusted.

Reflection Question:

How can you show more gentleness in your tone, body language, or reactions this week?

Couples Challenge:

Before responding to something frustrating today, pause and breathe a prayer for gentleness.

Prayer:

Lord, fill us with Your gentleness. Please help us respond with calm strength and create peace in our home. Amen.

Day Twenty One

Love that Reflects the Cross

Scripture: *Ephesians 5:25 (ESV) — "Husbands, love your wives, as Christ loved the church and gave himself up for her."*

Tyler stood quietly in the hospital room, watching his wife, Jen, sleep. The beeping of the monitors and the quiet hum of machines filled the space, a stark contrast to the whirlwind of the past few weeks. Jen's diagnosis had come fast and unexpected, pulling the rug out from under both of them.

She had always been the strong one, quick to laugh, full of energy, the one who kept their home running and their children grounded. But now, the roles had reversed. And every day since the diagnosis, Tyler had been learning what love really means.

He hadn't expected how exhausting it would be, learning her medications, attending every appointment, managing the kids' schedules while holding her hand through nausea and exhaustion. There were moments when he wanted to disappear for a while, just to avoid the weight of it all.

But each time he felt that pull, he remembered something deeper: love isn't about convenience. It's about commitment. It's about showing up when everything inside you want to run. Christ didn't go to the cross because it was easy — He went because He chose us.

Tyler tightened the blanket around Jen's shoulders and gently kissed her forehead. He had promised to love her in sickness and in health. And love, real love, the kind that reflects Jesus, means sacrificing when it's hard, staying when it would be easier to withdraw, serving without waiting to be thanked.

Later that night, as Jen stirred and reached for his hand, he was there. Still beside her. Not out of obligation, but because he had decided long ago that this was love: not just walking the aisle but walking with her through every valley.

Their marriage wasn't shining because life was perfect. It was shining because even in weakness, it reflected something stronger. A love that chooses. A love that stays. A love that looks like the cross.

Ephesians 5:25 calls husbands to love their wives as Christ loved the church and gave Himself up for her. That's not a casual or convenient kind of love — it's sacrificial, steadfast, and deeply intentional. It's the kind of love that shows up when everything in you wants to pull back. It's the kind of love that stays.

Tyler's story paints a powerful picture of this. His love for Jen wasn't proven in the easy seasons, but in the valley, when sickness came, when strength was tested, when the weight of caregiving felt overwhelming. In those moments, love became more than words or vows — it became action. It became sacrifice. And in that sacrifice, their marriage began to reflect something far greater than themselves. It began to reflect Christ.

> The cross defines what real love looks like. Jesus didn't choose us because we were easy to love — He chose us in our brokenness, and He stayed. That's the kind of love marriage is meant to mirror. Not a love that waits to be served, but one that serves first. Not a love that demands, but one that gives. Not a love that walks away when things get hard, but one that leans in even deeper.

When both spouses embrace this cross-shaped love, something beautiful happens. Pride gives way to humility. Bitterness is replaced by grace. And the union becomes more than just companionship — it becomes a living testimony of God's faithfulness.

Your marriage doesn't have to be perfect to be powerful. It just needs to reflect the love of Jesus, a love that chooses when it's hard, that stays when it's costly, and that gives when it's inconvenient. That kind of love is what makes a marriage shine, even in the darkest valleys. And that kind of love is what points the world to the One who first loved us.

Reflection Question:

What's one area of your marriage that needs more of Christ's self-giving love?

Couples Challenge:

Pray together at the foot of the cross and thank Jesus for His sacrifice and ask Him to shape your love after His.

Prayer:

Jesus, thank You for loving us first. Help our marriage reflect Your sacrificial love and bring glory to Your name. Amen.

WEEK FOUR

DAYS 22-28

THEME:

TRUST & TRANSPARENCY: BUILDING
SAFETY & HONESTY IN LOVE

KEY VERSE: PROVERBS 3:3
Let not steadfast love and faithfulness
forsake you; bind them around your neck;
write them on the tablet of your heart

Day Twenty Two

The Foundation of Trust

Scripture: *Psalm 37:3 (ESV) — "Trust in the Lord and do good; dwell in the land and befriend faithfulness."*

Samantha stood at the kitchen sink, staring out the window but not really seeing anything. Another long day had passed. Dishes were stacked, emails unanswered, and her heart felt just as cluttered as the counter. James was quiet again, retreating into his usual shell when life got overwhelming. She felt alone, not because he was gone, but because he was distant.

They hadn't had a real conversation in days. They moved around each other like two people sharing a schedule, not a marriage. Samantha wondered if the closeness they once had could ever return. She missed the way they used to laugh in the kitchen or talk late into the night. Now, they seemed to exist in parallel lanes, barely touching.

That night, after putting their daughter to bed, James came into the kitchen and saw her drying that same plate she'd already cleaned twice. He leaned on the counter and finally whispered, 'I know I haven't been present. I've just been trying to hold everything together in my own strength. And I don't even know when I stopped trusting that we don't have to do that alone.'

Samantha turned to face him. There were no dramatic accusations or eloquent speeches. Just quiet surrender. She nodded, and with tears brimming, said, 'Me too.'

Instead of circling around the same cycle of misunderstanding and silence, they made a different choice that night. They sat down, hands clasped across the table, and prayed for the first time in a long while, not for resolution, but for restoration.

From that night on, small changes flowed in. They didn't depend on a breakthrough feeling or force affection they didn't yet have. Instead, they chose faithfulness. They showed up. James started checking in more intentionally during the day. Samantha resisted the temptation to assume the worst during his quiet moments. They began to trust that even if the emotions weren't always loud, the commitment could still speak loudly.

Little by little, the safety returned. The honesty. The ease.

It wasn't dramatic or fast, but it was steady. It was a trust rebuilt not just in each other, but in the God who held them both, even when they couldn't hold each other very well.

Over time, their marriage became a place where truth didn't have to fight its way in, and promises weren't just made, but kept. Not because they were perfect, but because their hope was rooted deeper than circumstances. It was rooted in trust, not only in one another, but in the One who never fails.

Trust in marriage doesn't happen once, it's built choice by choice, moment by moment. It's strengthened by consistency and weakened by neglect. The good news? Trust can be rebuilt when both partners surrender their hearts to the Lord.

When you trust *God first*, you can better trust your spouse. Because you know, even if people fail, you're held by the One who never will. Faith in God steadies your love when fear or past wounds try to sabotage it.

Psalm 37:3 gives us a simple yet profound blueprint for life and love: *trust in the Lord, do good, dwell in the land, and befriend faithfulness*. In marriage, these words are more than poetic — they are deeply practical. They remind us that trust and faithfulness aren't one-time promises; they are daily decisions.

Samantha and James's story reflect what many couples quietly endure, emotional distance, unspoken weariness, and the slow drift that comes when life gets heavy and hearts grow tired. But what changed their trajectory wasn't a dramatic breakthrough; it was a quiet return to faithfulness, a decision to stop striving in their own strength and start trusting in God's.

Trust in marriage is built in the small, unseen moments: the text that says, 'I'm thinking of you,' the choice to listen instead of assuming, the prayer whispered when you feel disconnected. It's strengthened when both partners choose to show up, even when emotions feel flat or wounds are still healing. And when trust is rooted in God first, it becomes more resilient, because it's not built on the perfection of your spouse, but on the faithfulness of the One who never fails.

> When you trust the Lord, you stop trying to control outcomes and start inviting His peace into your relationship. You stop reacting out of fear and start responding with grace. That kind of trust creates space for healing, for truth to be spoken without fear, and for promises to be lived out with integrity.

Let your marriage be a place where trust is nurtured, not by perfection, but by presence, a place where faithfulness is not only expected but cherished. And remember, even if your love feels quiet, it can still be strong when it's anchored in a God who holds you both steady.

Let your marriage be a place where truth lives easily and promises are kept.

Reflection Question:

What helps you rebuild trust when it's been shaken?

Couples Challenge:

Talk about one area where trust could grow stronger and pray together for God's help to rebuild it.

Prayer:

Lord, You are faithful and true. Help us mirror Your trustworthiness in our words and actions toward each other. Amen.

DAY TWENTY THREE

Walking in Honesty

Scripture: *Ephesians 4:25 (ESV) — "Therefore, having put away falsehood, let each one of you speak the truth with his neighbor, for we are members one of another."*

Camille knew something was off, but she couldn't quite name it. Her husband, Darren, had been coming home later than usual, not extremely late, just enough to notice. He said work had gotten hectic. And maybe it had. But something in his tone, or how quickly he changed the subject, left a question lingering.

She didn't want to be the nagging wife. She told herself not to overthink it. So instead of asking directly, she got quieter. Less expressive. Less vulnerable. Inside, though, the space between them kept swelling. Small unspoken suspicions and growing fears took root in the silence.

It wasn't until a Saturday morning, when they sat across from each other at their favorite brunch spot, that Camille finally asked, in a voice more tired than accusatory, 'Is there something you're not telling me? Because I feel like I'm trying to connect with someone who's halfway gone.'

Darren looked down at his plate, then back at her. The pause felt like forever. Then came the truth, not scandalous, but significant.

He had been stressed, overwhelmed at work, and ashamed of how fragile he'd felt. Instead of talking to Camille about it, he buried himself in late hours and buried his emotions too. He confessed that he hadn't wanted her to see him as weak, so he hid behind vague explanations and worn-out excuses.

Camille listened, her heart pounding. Strangely, what she felt wasn't anger. It was relief. Not because everything was okay now, but because at least now, everything was real.

She reached across the table and said softly, 'I don't need you to be strong all the time. I need you to be honest. Even when it's messy.'

That moment cracked something open between them, not in a breaking way, but in a healing one. They began, together, to have conversations about things they used to avoid, anxieties, disappointments, insecurities, needs. It was uncomfortable at times but also freeing.

They learned that love doesn't deepen through perfection. It grows in the soil of truth. That honesty, even when it's vulnerable or uncomfortable, builds safety. That sharing what's real invites grace, not rejection.

Their marriage didn't magically become problem-free, but it became grounded, no longer shaped by assumptions or silence, but by the steady rhythm of openness, again and again.

Intimacy breathes best in the presence of truth. And love can only thrive where it's safe to be fully seen.

Ephesians 4:25 reminds us that truth is not optional in relationships — it's essential. When Paul says, 'having put away falsehood, let each one of you speak the truth with his neighbor,' he's not just talking about avoiding lies. He's calling us to live in honesty with one another, especially within the sacred bond of marriage.

Camille and Darren's story reveal how easy it is for distance to grow when truth is withheld, not through betrayal, but through silence. Darren didn't lie outright, but his emotional retreat created a gap that assumptions and fears quickly filled. Camille, unsure of what was real, began to withdraw, too. This is how intimacy begins to erode, not always through loud conflict, but through quiet disconnection.

Honesty is the oxygen of intimacy. Without it, love suffocates. And honesty doesn't just mean telling the truth when asked, it means offering your real self even when it's uncomfortable. It means saying, 'I'm not okay,' or 'I'm struggling,' or 'I need help,' not because you have it all together, but because you trust your spouse enough to let them in.

God calls couples to live in truth because deception, whether through lies, omissions, or emotional hiding, destroys connection. Secrets, half-truths, or emotional hiding create distance. But when you choose openness, even when it's messy, you invite grace. You create a space where love can grow deeper, not because everything is perfect, but because everything is real.

Honesty and humility go hand in hand. It takes humility to admit weakness, to confess failure, and to speak truthfully when it would be easier to pretend. But when both spouses commit to this kind of truth-telling, trust is built, safety is restored, and love becomes resilient.

Let your marriage be a place where truth lives easily, where neither person has to carry burdens alone or pretend to be someone they're not, because love thrives where it's safe to be fully seen. And that kind of safety starts with the courage to be honest.

Reflection Question:

Is there an area where you're tempted to hide rather than be honest with your spouse?

Couples Challenge:

Share something small but honest that's been on your heart lately. Practice gentle truth together.

Prayer:

Father, help us to walk in truth before You and before each other. Let our honesty be clothed in kindness and humility. Amen.

Day Twenty Four

When Trust Has Been Broken

Scripture: *Psalm 34:18 (ESV)* — *"The Lord is near to the brokenhearted and saves the crushed in spirit."*

Kara sat on the edge of the bed staring at the floor, her hands clenched in her lap. This is not how she imagined their tenth anniversary would start. A text message she wasn't supposed to see had changed everything, clear evidence that Ethan had been hiding things from her. Not an affair, but emotional conversations that had crossed boundaries, breaking sacred trust.

Ethan stood at the doorway, eyes heavy with regret. He hadn't tried to explain it away. For once, he hadn't used charm or half-measures. He simply said, 'I messed up. And I don't expect you to trust me today. But I'll spend as long as it takes rebuilding what I broke.'

Kara didn't have words. Her heart was too full of ache and confusion. But even in the pain, something in his posture, vulnerable, humble, told her he finally saw the weight of what he'd done.

The days that followed were not neat. Some mornings, Kara couldn't look at him. Other days, she found glimpses of the love they used to share. Instead of forcing forgiveness, they walked slowly. Ethan went to counseling and invited accountability. He gave Kara access to his world with nothing hidden. No pressure, just presence.

And Kara? She kept showing up, too, not out of obligation, but because somewhere deep in her soul, she felt the faintest whisper that something broken could be made whole again.

One evening, weeks later, they sat outside watching their kids chase fireflies. Ethan turned to her and quietly said, 'Thank you for seeing my repentance, even when trusting me again feels hard.'

She looked at him, tears in her eyes, but not from pain this time. 'I see how you're changing. It doesn't fix everything overnight, but it shows me you're doing the work.'

They both knew it would take more time. But they also knew healing was now in motion.

Their marriage didn't come back to life through a grand gesture, it resurrected in small moments: honest conversations, sincere apologies, boundaries respected, hearts surrendered.

Even when trust is shattered, it is not beyond repair. With God's help, what seemed dead can live again. Not as it was, but as something humbler, holier, and more deeply rooted in grace.

Few pains cut deeper than broken trust. Whether from betrayal, neglect, or disappointment, rebuilding feels impossible, but it isn't with God.

Healing takes time and truth. The one who broke trust must take full responsibility; the one who was hurt must allow space for repentance and renewal. Grace doesn't erase boundaries — it rebuilds them with God's wisdom and patience.

Psalm 34:18 reminds us that the Lord is near to the brokenhearted and saves those who are crushed in spirit. In the aftermath of broken trust, this truth becomes more than a comforting verse — it becomes a lifeline. When trust is betrayed, whether through emotional infidelity, deception, or neglect, the pain can feel unbearable. But God doesn't turn away from our heartbreak. He draws near. And in His nearness, there is hope.

Kara and Ethan's story shows that healing is not about quick fixes or sweeping things under the rug. It's about facing the pain honestly, allowing space for true repentance, and choosing to walk slowly toward restoration. Ethan didn't demand forgiveness, he demonstrated change. Kara didn't offer instant trust, she offered presence. And in that sacred in-between, God began to rebuild what had been broken.

Rebuilding trust is a process that requires both truth and time. The one who broke it must be willing to own the damage without excuses, and the one who was hurt must be given the freedom to feel, process, and heal without pressure. Grace is not a shortcut past pain, it is the strength to endure it together, with God leading the way.

Boundaries, accountability, and transparency are not signs of distrust — they are tools of wisdom in the rebuilding process. True repentance welcomes those things, not as punishment, but as part of the healing. And while the road is long, every step taken in humility and faith brings you closer to restoration.

Jesus is the healer of broken things. He doesn't just patch up our pain — He resurrects what we thought was lost. When both hearts surrender to Him, even the most devastated marriage can find new life, not as it was before, but as something deeper, more honest, and more dependent on His grace.

So, if you're walking through the pain of broken trust, know this: with God, healing is possible. Not overnight. Not without effort. But with truth, humility, and the nearness of the Lord, what's been shattered can be made whole again. What's dead can live again when both hearts surrender to Him.

Reflection Question:

What step could you take today, small or big, toward rebuilding trust in your marriage?

Couples Challenge:

Write down one way you can help restore trust in your relationship this week and pray over it together.

Prayer:

Lord, heal the broken places between us. Restore what's been lost and teach us to walk in grace, patience, and truth. Amen.

Day Twenty Five

Vulnerability: The Doorway to Intimacy

Scripture: *2 Corinthians 12:9 (ESV) — "My grace is sufficient for you, for my power is made perfect in weakness."*

Joel had always been the steady one. The calm voice in the storm, the planner, the provider. He prided himself on being dependable, someone his wife Kayla could count on. But lately, underneath his steady tone and rehearsed smiles, there was a quiet unraveling. Work was overwhelming, financial pressures weighed heavier than he let on, and an old fear of failure had crept in, whispering lies at the back of his mind.

But he didn't share that. He tucked it away, thinking he was protecting Kayla, thinking that strength meant silence.

Kayla, however, could feel the distance growing. His voice was short, his laugh was rare, and even when they were in the same room, she felt alone. One evening, after he brushed off yet another 'I'm fine,' she gently placed her hand on his arm and said, 'Joel, I don't need the version of you that has it all together. I need the real you, even if that version is tired, unsure, or barely holding on.'

Her words cracked something open in him.

He sat down and exhaled, really exhaled, for the first time in weeks. And there, in the quiet of their little kitchen, he let the mask fall. He talked. About the fear he felt of failing her. About how exhausting it was pretending he was okay, about how he felt like he had to be strong all the time, or he'd somehow be letting her down.

Kayla didn't flinch. She listened. She nodded. Then she whispered, 'Your weakness doesn't scare me. It draws me closer. I'm not looking for perfect — I'm looking for present.'

From that moment on, something shifted in their marriage. Not dramatically, not all at once, but beautifully. Joel started asking for prayer instead of pretending he didn't need it. Kayla began to share her own fears and dreams more freely, seeing that honesty was met not with judgment but grace.

They built a rhythm of checking in, not just about the tasks of life, but the state of each other's hearts. Vulnerability became not something to avoid, but a doorway to deeper connection.

They discovered that intimacy doesn't grow in polished moments, but in shared weakness, when the masks fall and grace rises. And in the safety of that kind of love, they found their truest strength.

2 Corinthians 12:9 reminds us that God's grace is not just sufficient — it is made perfect in our weakness. That means our struggles, our limitations, and our vulnerability are not liabilities in God's eyes. They are the very places where His strength shows up the clearest. And in marriage, those moments of weakness can become the most powerful opportunities for connection.

Joel's story is a reminder that strength isn't found in pretending everything is fine. It's found in the courage to be real. He thought he was protecting Kayla by hiding his stress and fear, but in reality, the silence was creating distance between them. It wasn't until he allowed himself to be seen, really seen, that their relationship began to deepen.

Real closeness requires real openness. Vulnerability means letting your spouse see the parts of you that aren't polished, the fears, insecurities, and dreams you usually keep tucked away. It's scary, yes. But it's also sacred. Because when we choose to open up, we invite our spouse not just into our lives, but into our hearts.

God designed marriage to be a safe place for that kind of honesty. When you share your weakness, you don't lose respect, you build intimacy. You show that you trust your spouse enough to lay down the mask. And in that space, love grows deeper, stronger, more authentic.

The walls we build to protect ourselves often end up isolating us. But grace thrives where masks fall. When we stop performing and start being present, we create a rhythm of trust. A rhythm where prayer replaces pressure, and presence replaces perfection.

In your marriage, don't be afraid to let your guard down. Because when both of you bring your real selves to the table, you give each other the gift of grace. And in that grace, God's power is made perfect, not in your strength, but in your surrender.

Reflection Question:

What keeps you from being completely open with your spouse, and how might you start breaking that wall down?

Couples Challenge:

Each of you share one personal fear or insecurity you rarely talk about. Listen with grace, not advice.

Prayer:

Jesus, help us be honest about our hearts and safe for each other's vulnerability. Let grace deepen our intimacy. Amen.

DAY TWENTY SIX

Keeping Promises

Scripture: *Numbers 30:2 (ESV)* — *"If a man vows a vow to the Lord... he shall not break his word. He shall do according to all that proceeds out of his mouth."*

Ellie still remembered the day Andrew stood before their friends and family and promised to love her through everything, the joy and the mess, the beauty and the hard. At the time, it had all felt so grand and romantic. But now, eight years later, 'everything' had come to mean diaper blowouts at 2 a.m., medical bills they hadn't expected, and a million ordinary decisions that never made it onto anyone's highlight reel.

One Wednesday afternoon, she was feeling frayed. Their toddler had been sick for days, and Andrew had been working overtime to meet a deadline. That morning, as he hurried out the door, he had kissed her cheek and said, 'I'll be home by six so you can take a break. I promise.'

By 5:55, she told herself not to get frustrated. By 5:59, her resolve started began to bend. But at exactly 5:59, the front door creaked open. Andrew walked in, looking like he'd sprinted from the car. He was still in his wrinkled work shirt, hair windblown, and holding a bag with her favorite takeout.

'Traffic was awful,' he said, hugging her as their toddler squealed from the living room. 'But I told you I'd be home. And I meant it.'

Ellie felt something simple but revealing settle in her heart. It wasn't about the food or even the exact time on the clock, it was about the reliability of his word. That even in the chaos, even when rushed or tired, he had remembered what he said. His follow-through gave her more than rest that night — it gave her assurance.

Over the years, it wasn't just the big vows they'd made on their wedding day that held them together. It was the small promises kept, picking up milk on the way home because he said he would, checking in during a tough day, showing up when it wasn't convenient. Each followed-through word formed a thread of trust that wrapped around their relationship like an anchor.

Ellie later told a friend, 'It's not about perfection. It's about showing up when you say you will. It's about keeping the little things sacred. That's where our marriage feels safest.'

Promises, they had learned, weren't just made once. They were kept, over and over. Quietly. Faithfully. And in each kept promise, their love reflected the One whose promises never fail.

Promises are sacred because they mirror God's own character. Marriage vows weren't meant to be poetic words for one day — they're anchors for every day.

Numbers 30:2 reminds us that when we make a vow, especially before the Lord, we are called to keep it. In marriage, those vows are not just ceremonial words spoken on a beautiful day, they are sacred commitments meant to carry us through every ordinary and difficult moment that follows.

Ellie and Andrew's story is a beautiful reminder that love is built not only on grand gestures but on consistent faithfulness. When Andrew showed up, disheveled, tired, but right on time, he wasn't just fulfilling a promise to help with the baby. He was reinforcing the foundation of trust in their marriage. His reliability in that small moment spoke volumes: You can count on me. I meant what I said.

> Promises in marriage matter because they reflect the character of God, who always keeps His word. When we follow through on our commitments, even the small ones, we mirror His faithfulness. Every time you show up when you said you would, follow through on a task, or simply honor your word, you are saying to your spouse, 'You are safe with me. I won't let my words be empty.'

Keeping promises creates a culture of trust in the relationship. It tells your spouse that they don't have to wonder or second guess, they can rest in your word. And this kind of integrity doesn't require perfection; it requires consistency. It's not about never being late or never forgetting, it's about doing your best to honor what you've said and making it right when you fall short.

In a world where words are often cheap and commitments are easily broken, a marriage built on kept promises stands as a powerful testimony. It shows that love is more than emotion, it's a decision, repeated daily. And every kept promise, no matter how small, becomes a thread in the fabric of lasting love, woven in the likeness of the God who never fails to keep His.

Reflection Question:

What's one commitment you could renew to strengthen trust in your marriage today?

Couples Challenge:

Each of you reaffirm one promise, spoken or unspoken, that you want to honor this week intentionally.

Prayer:

Lord, make us people of our word. Strengthen our integrity and remind us that every promise reflects Your faithfulness. Amen.

Day Twenty Seven

Guarding Each Other's Confidence

Scripture: *Proverbs 11:13 (ESV)* — *"Whoever goes about slandering reveals secrets, but he who is trustworthy in spirit keeps a thing covered."*

Jason sat on the couch, scrolling through his phone, when he heard his wife, Mia, coming down the stairs. Her footsteps were slower than usual, and when she walked into the room, her eyes looked heavy.

She sat beside him and exhaled. 'I've been trying to act like everything's fine, but it's not. I've been struggling with anxiety for weeks, and I feel like I'm failing at everything, work, parenting, all of it.'

Jason turned toward her, surprised by the confession. Mia had always been the strong one, the calm in their storm. He listened quietly, knowing how hard it was for her to admit weakness.

That night, he didn't try to fix anything. He just listened. He thanked her for trusting him. And when she gently asked him to keep it between them, not to share it with anyone, not even close friends, he promised he would.

A few days later, Jason was at a backyard barbecue with some friends. The conversation turned to how hard parenting and marriage could be, and one friend joked, 'Come on, you're telling me your wife doesn't lose it once in a while, too?'

Jason thought for a second. He could have shared that Mia had been struggling, not in cruelty, just in conversation. But something inside him paused. He remembered her eyes from that night. The trust behind her words. The unspoken question: 'Is it safe to let you see this part of me?'

He smiled and simply said, 'We all have our moments, but I'm grateful for how strong we are together.'

Later that week, Mia sat beside him again during a quiet evening and said, 'You know, I don't feel as anxious when I talk to you anymore. There's peace in just being heard.'

What she didn't know was that Jason had chosen, every time, to guard her heart like sacred ground. Her fears, spoken in confidence, were never passed around. Not even in harmless anecdotes or subtle hints.

That trust built something deep between them. She began sharing more, and he began listening with more intention. She knew she had a partner who not only heard her heart but also protected it.

Over the years, they built a quiet strength not just from love but also from loyalty, not just from support, but from safety.

In marriage, what's shared in vulnerability should be held in reverence. And when your spouse knows that their secrets are safe, their soul begins to feel just as secure.

Proverbs 11:13 teaches us that trustworthiness is shown not just in what we say, but in what we choose not to say. In marriage, this principle becomes deeply personal. When your spouse shares something vulnerable, a fear, a failure, a private struggle, they are placing a piece of their heart in your hands. How you handle that moment determines whether trust deepens or erodes.

Jason's decision to protect Mia's confession, even in a casual conversation with friends, was more than just discretion — it was love in action. He understood that what she shared wasn't just information; it was an invitation into her inner world. And by keeping it sacred, he gave her something rare and powerful: safety.

Trust grows when your spouse knows their heart is safe with you. Guarding their confidence means protecting their private words, not using them against them in a future argument, and not turning their pain into a story for others, even if it seems harmless. Never use them as weapons or share them for gossip. What's shared in vulnerability should be held in reverence.

Marriage is sacred ground. It's a space where both people should feel free to be fully known without fear of exposure or betrayal. When you honor that space, when you choose not to share what was entrusted to you, you nurture deep emotional security. You create a climate where honesty can flourish, where defenses can drop, and where true intimacy can grow.

This kind of loyalty builds a bond that goes beyond affection — it builds assurance. Your spouse will feel more confident to share their heart, knowing it won't be mishandled. And in that atmosphere of trust and protection, love becomes not just something you feel, but something you can count on.

Reflection Question:

Can your spouse trust that what they tell you in confidence will stay between you and God?

Couples Challenge:

Recommit today to protecting each other's privacy in words, conversations, and online behavior.

Prayer:

Father, help us to honor each other's hearts. Make our marriage a refuge of trust where love feels safe and protected. Amen.

Day Twenty Eight

Trusting God Together

Scripture: *Isaiah 26:3–4 (ESV) — "You keep him in perfect peace whose mind is stayed on you, because he trusts in you. Trust in the Lord forever, for the Lord God is an everlasting rock."*

Molly and Caleb had always been planners. From the day they got married, they had a timeline in mind, when they'd buy a house, when to start a family, when to take that long-awaited trip to Europe. But when Caleb lost his job unexpectedly, their carefully mapped-out future blurred overnight.

At first, they tried to stay positive. 'It's just a setback,' Molly told herself. But as weeks turned into months, the numbers in their bank account grew smaller, and the tension between them grew louder. Every conversation seemed to end with a question neither of them could answer: 'What are we going to do?'

One evening, after another round of unpaid bills sat unopened on the counter, Caleb sat silently on the porch, his shoulders slumped. Molly sat beside him, fighting tears of her own. He looked at her and said, 'I feel like I've failed us. I don't know how to fix this.'

Molly took a shaky breath, then reached for his hand. 'We don't have to fix this alone. Maybe that's where we've been going wrong, trying to muscle our way through what only God can carry.'

That night, instead of rehearsing worst-case scenarios or digging back into job postings, they prayed together for the first time in weeks. Not a polished prayer, not a perfect plan, just an honest cry for peace, for provision, for clarity.

Something shifted.

They didn't find a job the next day. Their finances didn't magically improve. But their fear began to fade. Each morning, they started praying before anything else. They talked through decisions with an open Bible nearby. When one of them wavered, the other stood firm. When both felt uncertain, they leaned on trust deeper than their own understanding.

Caleb eventually found work. It wasn't the job they had hoped for, but it was good, solid ground. By then, they had already built something more valuable than a perfect plan, they had built peace rooted in God, not circumstances.

Years later, Molly would look back at that season not with bitterness, but with quiet gratitude. Because in the storm that could have torn them apart, they found an anchor that held them together.

When trust between them felt shaken, trust in God steadied their steps. And because of that, their marriage grew not just stronger, but unshakable.

The most stable marriages are built on a shared foundation of trust in *God*. When both of you anchor your faith in Him, you'll weather every storm with peace.

Isaiah 26:3–4 reminds us of a consistent truth: perfect peace isn't found in perfect circumstances, but in a steadfast heart that trusts in the Lord. For Molly and Caleb, that truth became their anchor when everything else felt uncertain. Their plans unraveled, their security was shaken, and even their confidence in each other wavered under the weight of stress and fear. But when they shifted their focus from the problem to the Provider, peace began to take root.

When trust in each other felt fragile, trust in God steadied their hearts. And because of that, their marriage didn't just survive the storm, it was strengthened by it. That's the power of a shared faith. When both spouses look to God as their source and foundation, they stop trying to carry the full weight of life alone. They learn to lean on the One who never fails.

> The most stable marriages are not built on flawless plans or uninterrupted success. They are built on a shared dependence on God. When a couple prays together, seeks His wisdom together, and chooses to trust Him together, they become unshakable, not because life is easy, but because their foundation is strong.

Life's uncertainties, like job loss, medical diagnoses, or unexpected detours, don't have to divide you. In fact, they can draw you closer when you face them hand in hand, anchored in faith. Praying together becomes more than a spiritual habit; it becomes a lifeline. Planning together becomes more than strategy; it becomes surrender.

When trust in each other wavers, trust in God will steady you. He is the everlasting Rock, and when your marriage is built on Him, you won't be easily moved. Peace doesn't come from knowing the outcome, it comes from knowing the One who holds your future. And when you stand on that truth together, you'll find that even the hardest seasons can lead to the deepest unity.

Reflection Question:

Where do you need to trust God together more fully in this season?

Couples Challenge:

Hold hands and pray together about one area of uncertainty. Release control and place it in God's hands.

Prayer:

Lord, You are our Rock and Refuge. Teach us to trust You together through every joy and trial. Strengthen our unity through shared faith in You. Amen.

WEEK FIVE

DAYS 29-35

THEME:

INTIMACY & ONENESS: RECLAIMING
CONNECTION IN HEART, MIND, & BODY

KEY VERSE:
1 CORINTHIANS 7:4

For the wife does not have authority over her
own body, but the husband does. Likewise
the husband does not have authority over his
own body, but the wife does

DAY TWENTY NINE

God's Blueprint for Oneness

Scripture: *Mark 10:9 (ESV) — "What therefore God has joined together, let not man separate."*

It was a quiet Saturday morning when Zac and Alina found themselves standing in the middle of their cluttered garage, surrounded by boxes they had promised to unpack months ago. The sun streamed through the small window, casting light on the dust motes floating in the air. What started as a simple task quickly turned into a disagreement, one of those seemingly small arguments that somehow carried the weight of many unspoken frustrations.

Zac wanted to sort and donate. Alina wanted to keep and organize. Voices rose, patience thinned, and before long, they stood on opposite sides of the garage, both silent, both hurt.

Later that day, Zac sat alone on the front steps, watching the wind sway the branches of the old oak tree. He thought about the early days of their marriage, the laughter, the long walks, the dreams they once painted in bright colors. Somewhere along the way, those moments had been crowded out by schedules, responsibilities, and silent assumptions.

Alina joined him quietly, offering a cup of coffee without a word. They sat for a while, the silence now softer, more open. Finally, Zac spoke.

'This isn't about boxes, is it?'

Alina shook her head, her eyes misty. 'I miss us.'

He reached for her hand, and they sat there, fingers entwined, remembering that their marriage wasn't built on shared tasks, but on shared hearts. They prayed together right there on the steps, asking God to help them protect what He had joined, not just the vows they had spoken, but the oneness He had designed.

That evening, they returned to the garage, not to finish a chore, but to begin again, not as two people trying to win a disagreement, but as one couple determined to fight for unity. They laughed more, listened better, and held each other longer.

The world might have seen a couple sorting through old boxes. But heaven saw something sacred, two hearts choosing oneness, again.

Marriage is God's idea, and His design for it is deeper than partnership, it's *oneness*. That doesn't mean sameness; it means two distinct people joined into one covenant, physically, emotionally, and spiritually.

Marriage is more than a contract; it is a covenant designed and initiated by God Himself. When Jesus said in Mark 10:9, 'What therefore God has joined together, let not man separate,' He wasn't just giving a warning, He was revealing a divine truth. God is the One who joins a husband and wife, and that union is sacred. It's not merely about living under the same roof or sharing responsibilities. It's about becoming one in spirit, heart, and purpose.

The story of Zac and Alina illustrates how easily the clutter of life, both literal and emotional, can wedge its way into a marriage. What begins as a disagreement over boxes can uncover deeper misalignments, unmet expectations, and unspoken needs. But it also shows the beauty of choosing oneness again. When they paused, reflected, and prayed, they realigned their hearts with God's design.

Biblically, oneness in marriage reflects the unity within the Trinity, distinct persons, yet perfectly united. Ephesians 5:31-32 echoes this mystery, stating that marriage points to Christ and the Church. This means every time a couple chooses unity over division, they reflect God's love story to the world.

Intimacy, as God defines it, is not just about physical closeness, but about spiritual and emotional connection. It's about knowing and being known, loving and being loved, even in moments of tension or disappointment. Protecting that kind of intimacy takes intentionality, through prayer, honest communication, regular forgiveness, and genuine affection.

> The enemy of oneness is often subtle. It can be busyness that keeps couples too tired to connect, bitterness that builds from unresolved conflicts, or distractions that shift focus away from each other. But when couples recognize these threats and actively guard against them, they honor what God has joined.

Let the garage moments of life, those ordinary, messy, frustrating times, become sacred opportunities to choose each other again. Not because it's easy, but because it's holy. When you fight for oneness, you're not just preserving a relationship; you're participating in a divine design that reflects the heart of God.

The world defines intimacy as pleasure; God defines it as purpose, a reflection of His unity and love. When you protect oneness through prayer, communication, forgiveness, and affection, you protect something sacred.

Don't let anything, busyness, bitterness, or distraction, pull apart what God has joined together.

Reflection Question:
What has been threatening your sense of "oneness" lately and how can you guard it better?

Couples Challenge:
Talk about one thing that helps you feel most connected as a couple and commit to doing it this week.

Prayer:
Lord, thank You for joining us together as one. Help us fiercely guard our unity and cherish the covenant You created. Amen.

Day Thirty

Emotional Intimacy: Being Fully Known

Scripture: *1 John 4:18 (ESV)* — *"There is no fear in love, but perfect love casts out fear."*

It was just after dinner when Mary noticed the distance in Larry's eyes again. He was there, physically, helping clear the dishes, asking about her day, but something in his voice felt rehearsed, like a script he had memorized. They had been married for eight years, and lately, their conversations had become more about logistics than life.

She hesitated, drying her hands on a towel, then turned to him.

'Are you okay? Really?'

Larry paused, the question hanging heavier than the silence that followed. He looked down, then slowly leaned against the counter.

'I don't know,' he admitted. 'Work's been overwhelming, and I've been feeling like I'm failing at everything. I didn't want to say anything because I didn't want to disappoint you.'

Mary stepped closer, her heart aching. 'You could never disappoint me by being honest. I'd rather know your fears than pretend everything's fine.'

He looked up, eyes searching hers for judgment, but found only compassion. And in that moment, something shifted. The walls he had quietly built began to crumble, not because she pried them down, but because she stood close enough for him to feel safe.

They sat on the couch that night, not to watch a show or scroll through phones, but to talk, really talk. About the pressure he felt to provide, about her quiet fears of being emotionally alone, about the dreams they had shelved for someday.

Tears came. So did laughter. And in the middle of their imperfect words, they rediscovered something sacred, a love that didn't demand perfection, only presence.

That night, they didn't solve every problem or erase every worry. But they did something more important: they chose to be emotionally available, honest, and to stay close, not just in body, but in heart.

And that kind of love? It cast out fear.

Intimacy begins long before touch — it starts with emotional safety. When you can be honest without fear of rejection, you experience the kind of love that frees instead of frightens.

1 John 4:18 reminds us that 'There is no fear in love, but perfect love casts out fear.' This verse doesn't just apply to our relationship with God — it also speaks powerfully to how we love each other in marriage. Fear and love cannot thrive in the same space. When fear creeps in, fear of rejection, fear of failure, fear of not being enough, it builds walls. But love, especially God-shaped love, tear down those walls.

In Mary and Larry's story, we see how emotional distance can quietly grow between two people who still love each other deeply. It wasn't a lack of affection or commitment; it was the absence of emotional safety. Larry didn't feel free to share his struggles because he was afraid of disappointing Mary. That fear created a quiet barrier between them, until Mary responded with compassion instead of criticism.

Emotional intimacy begins with safety. It's not just about being physically close, but about being fully known and still fully loved. When a spouse feels safe enough to say, 'I'm not okay,' and is met with grace instead of judgment, that's where true intimacy begins. That's what perfect love does, it doesn't demand performance, it invites presence.

> Many couples drift not because of a significant crisis, but because they stop sharing what's real. Over time, conversations become transactional, about schedules, chores, and responsibilities, and the heart-level connection fades. But love that reflects God's heart is a love that listens, that asks deeper questions, and that stays present even when the answers are messy.

Perfect love in marriage doesn't mean getting everything right. It means showing up, emotionally, spiritually, and relationally. It means being willing to sit on the couch and talk about fears, not just finances. It means choosing to be vulnerable, even when it's uncomfortable, and choosing to respond with grace when your spouse opens up.

Let this be a reminder: your spouse doesn't need you to be perfect. They need you to be present. They need to know that when they share their heart, they're safe. And when that kind of love is practiced daily, fear loses its grip, and true intimacy takes root.

Perfect love isn't about perfection; it's about presence. Stay emotionally available, even when it's hard.

Reflection Question:

What fears or insecurities make it difficult for you to be emotionally vulnerable?

Couples Challenge:

Spend 10 minutes tonight sharing something you've been feeling lately without problem-solving, just listening.

Prayer:

Jesus, teach us to love without fear. Help us open our hearts fully to one another, just as You open Yours to us. Amen.

Day Thirty One

Spiritual Intimacy: Growing Together in Christ

Scripture: *Ecclesiastes 4:12 (ESV) — "A threefold cord is not quickly broken."*

It was a rainy Sunday morning when Harold and Tessa found themselves sitting side by side on the edge of their bed, holding hands in silence. The night before had ended in another argument, not loud or explosive, but the kind that left a lingering ache. Misunderstandings had piled up, and both felt weary.

They had tried talking it out, but the words only seemed to deepen the divide. Now, with the sound of rain tapping against the window, Harold finally whispered, 'Maybe we need more than just us.'

Tessa nodded, her eyes brimming with tears. 'We've been trying to fix this on our own. But maybe we're missing the One who holds us together.'

That morning, instead of going through their usual routine, they knelt beside the bed and prayed, not polished prayers, just raw, honest words. They asked God to soften their hearts, to help them listen better, to love deeper. It felt awkward at first, but something shifted as they prayed. The tension began to lift, and in its place came peace, not because every issue was solved, but because they had invited God into the center.

Later that week, they started reading a short devotional together each morning, just a few minutes before the day began. They prayed before dinner, not out of habit, but from a growing desire to stay connected, not only to each other but to the One who was now anchoring them.

They began to see their struggles differently. Instead of blaming each other, they started facing challenges as a team. When one felt weak, the other reminded them of God's strength. When life pulled them in different directions, they found their way back through shared faith.

What once felt fragile began to feel strong, not because they were perfect, but because they were united in something greater than themselves. Their love was no longer just about compatibility or effort. It was about surrender, to each other, and to God.

And in that sacred space, spiritual intimacy grew. Their hearts became not just joined but woven together with the thread of grace.

The strongest marriages have Christ woven through the center. Spiritual intimacy grows when couples pursue God together, praying, worshiping, reading Scripture, and serving side by side.

When you seek Him as one, your unity deepens. You start seeing challenges as shared missions instead of personal battles. God becomes not just your witness but your anchor.

Ecclesiastes 4:12 reminds us that a threefold cord is not quickly broken. This verse is often quoted in the context of marriage, and for good reason. A relationship between two people is significantly strengthened when it is intertwined with a third strand, God Himself. Harold and Tessa's story is a beautiful illustration of this truth. Despite their love and best intentions, they found themselves weary and disconnected. Their efforts alone weren't enough. But when they turned to God together, something shifted.

This is the power of spiritual intimacy. It is more than attending church together or saying grace before meals. It is the intentional pursuit of God as a couple, a shared spiritual journey that binds hearts in a way nothing else can. When couples pray together, worship together, and seek God's Word together, they open the door for God not only to guide their relationship but also to sustain it.

> In marriage, challenges are inevitable. But when Christ is at the center, those challenges become opportunities to grow closer instead of reasons to drift apart. Instead of facing struggles as adversaries, spiritually connected couples face them as a unified team, anchored in God's grace and truth.

Spiritual intimacy doesn't require perfection. It begins with simple steps, a prayer whispered together, a verse read before bed, a moment of worship shared in the car. These small habits create space for God to dwell in the relationship, and over time, they build a foundation that can weather any storm.

The beauty of a Christ-centered marriage is that it's not just about what you can do for each other, but about what God can do in and through you as one. When you invite Him into your relationship, you don't just grow closer to Him, you grow closer to each other. That's where true oneness begins, and that's where lasting love is sustained.

Reflection Question:

How consistent are you in seeking God together, and what helps or hinders that rhythm?

Couples Challenge:

Pray together out loud tonight, even a short prayer of gratitude or surrender.

Prayer:

Lord, make us one in spirit and truth. Draw us close to You and closer to each other as we seek Your presence daily. Amen.

Day Thirty Two

Physical Intimacy: God's Good Design

Scripture: *1 Corinthians 7:3–4 (ESV) — "The husband should give to his wife her conjugal rights, and likewise the wife to her husband."*

It had been a quiet tension lingering between them for weeks — not spoken but felt. Chastity noticed that Bill avoided eye contact when they passed in the hallway. He saw how she always seemed too tired, too distracted, too distant. Their conversations had become practical, their routines efficient. But the warmth, the closeness, especially the physical connection, had faded.

One night, after the kids were asleep and the house had finally settled, Chastity sat at the edge of the bed, her heart heavy. She glanced at Bill, who was sitting with his back against the headboard, scrolling through his phone. She took a breath and spoke softly.

'Can we talk?'

He looked up, surprised but attentive. She hesitated, then continued, 'I miss us. Not just the way things used to be physically, but the way we used to feel safe with each other. I don't want us to drift any further.'

Bill set his phone aside, his expression softening. 'I miss us too. I've been afraid to bring it up because I didn't want to make you feel pressured. But the distance... It's been hard.'

They sat in silence for a moment, not out of discomfort but out of reflection. Then Chastity reached for his hand.

'What if we prayed about it together? Not just for the physical part of our marriage, but for the emotional closeness we've lost.'

Bill nodded, and together they bowed their heads, asking God to heal the places where hurt had settled, to restore tenderness where walls had formed, and to help them love each other selflessly, in every way.

Over the following days, something began to change. They started being more intentional, small touches, kind words, longer hugs. They talked more openly about their needs and fears. And slowly, their physical intimacy began to return, not as a duty or obligation, but as a sacred expression of love and trust.

It wasn't perfect, but it was real. And in that renewed connection, they discovered something deeper, that physical intimacy, when rooted in emotional safety and mutual care, is not just about desire. It's about giving. It's about honoring. And it's about worshiping the God who brought them together in the first place.

1 Corinthians 7:3–4 reminds us that physical intimacy in marriage is not only a gift but also a responsibility, one that flows from love, not obligation. In a culture that often distorts or devalues sex, Scripture reclaims it as something sacred. God designed physical intimacy to be an expression of covenant love, not just a physical act, but a spiritual and emotional connection that reflects His unity design.

Chastity and Bill's story captures a reality many couples face at some point: emotional and physical distance that creeps in quietly, often unnoticed until it becomes a wall. Their willingness to talk openly, to pray together, and to seek healing shows the heart of biblical intimacy, one that is rooted in mutual care, emotional safety, and selfless love.

> Physical intimacy in marriage is not dirty or shameful — it is divine. It is a holy act when shared in the context of love, trust, and covenant. When approached with tenderness and respect, it becomes more than just a response to desire; it becomes an act of worship, a way to honor God by honoring each other.

But true intimacy cannot thrive in an environment of pressure or fear. It must be nurtured through emotional connection, honest communication, and mutual giving. As 1 Corinthians 7 teaches, both husband and wife are called to give to one another, not to demand, but to serve. This kind of love mirrors Christ, who gives Himself fully and sacrificially.

If this area of your marriage has grown distant or strained, don't ignore it or carry the weight alone. Bring it before God together. Pray for healing, for renewed desire, for deeper connection. God delights in restoring what feels broken and reviving what has grown cold. He is not ashamed of your need for closeness — He created it.

Let your physical relationship be a reflection of something greater, a love that gives, that honors, and that points back to the One who joined you together. In that sacred space, intimacy becomes more than just closeness, it becomes communion.

If this area of your marriage has been distant, pray together for healing and renewed closeness. God delights in restoring what's been strained.

Reflection Question:

What helps you feel most loved and connected physically and how can you communicate that with grace?

Couples Challenge:

Have an honest, kind conversation about your physical connection, no judgment, just curiosity and care.

Prayer:

Father, thank You for the gift of intimacy. Help us honor You with our bodies and build a connection that reflects Your pure love. Amen.

Day Thirty Three

Protecting Intimacy from Distraction

Scripture: *Song of Solomon 2:15 (ESV)* — *"Catch the foxes for us, the little foxes that spoil the vineyards."*

Tom and Marissa used to have Friday nights all to themselves. It was their sacred rhythm, dinner at their favorite spot, long walks, and conversations that drifted late into the evening. But lately, Friday nights had become just like every other night, filled with work emails, laundry piles, and the hum of a TV playing in the background while they sat on opposite ends of the couch, each scrolling through their phones.

One evening, Marissa looked over and realized she couldn't remember the last time they had laughed together, really laughed. She missed the way Tom used to reach for her hand without thinking, the way he used to ask about her dreams, as if they still mattered. She felt the ache of distance, even though he was sitting just a few feet away.

The next morning, she brought it up gently over coffee.

'I miss us,' she said, stirring her cup slowly. 'I feel like we've let life sneak in and steal our time.'

Tom looked up, his expression softening. He nodded slowly. 'I know. I've felt it too. It's like we've been surviving instead of connecting.'

They talked, really talked, for the first time in weeks. No distractions, no multitasking, just honesty. Together, they decided to make changes. They set a weekly date night again, even if it was just a walk or a homemade dinner with phones turned off. They agreed to put their devices away after 8 p.m., to protect their evenings as sacred time. And they promised to check in emotionally, not just logistically.

It wasn't about grand gestures. It was about guarding the little things, the small moments that had once made their love grow. They started noticing each other again, appreciating the everyday kindnesses that had gone unnoticed. Laughter returned. So did affection.

Their marriage finally began to breathe again. What had once been overrun with the weeds of distraction was being tended with intention. And in that careful, consistent love, their garden began to bloom once more.

The "little foxes", busyness, fatigue, technology, unresolved tension, can quietly destroy connection. Most marriages don't lose intimacy in a moment; they lose it through neglect. Protecting intimacy means being intentional. Set boundaries around phone time, prioritize date nights, and keep pursuing each other.

Song of Solomon 2:15 gives us a powerful visual: 'Catch the foxes for us, the little foxes that spoil the vineyards.' In the context of marriage, this verse reminds us that it's often not the big, dramatic moments that erode intimacy, it's the small, subtle things that go unnoticed and unchecked. Just like tiny foxes can ruin a vineyard by nibbling at the roots, small habits and distractions can quietly damage the foundation of a relationship.

Tom and Marissa's story is one many couples can relate to. They didn't fall out of love — they simply drifted. Life got busy. Screens replaced conversations. Fatigue replaced connection. And before they realized it, the closeness they once cherished had been replaced by routine and distance. But their story also shows the power of awareness and intentionality. When they recognized the drift and chose to act, they began to restore what had been lost, not through grand gestures, but through small, consistent choices to reconnect.

Biblically, marriage is often compared to a garden, a place that requires tending, pruning, and protection. Love doesn't thrive on autopilot. It needs intentional time, focused attention, and emotional investment. Protecting intimacy means catching the little foxes early, things like constant phone use, unchecked stress, unresolved tension, or simply the habit of coexisting without connecting.

Being intentional might look like setting a regular date night, even if it's simple. It might mean turning off devices during dinner or asking deeper questions instead of sticking to surface-level updates. It means noticing each other again, choosing to see, to listen, to pursue, even in the middle of busy seasons.

Your marriage is a vineyard. If you want it to flourish, you have to guard it. Protect your time and attention as sacred spaces where love can grow freely. Don't wait for a crisis to reconnect. Start with the small things, because the little foxes may be small, but so are the seeds of restoration. And with God's help, those seeds can bring your love back to life.

Guard your time and attention as sacred spaces where love grows freely.

Reflection Question:

What "little foxes" have been spoiling your intimacy lately, and how can you deal with them together?

Couples Challenge:

Choose one practical boundary this week to protect your connection (e.g., no phones in bed, a weekly date night).

Prayer:

Lord, help us guard our intimacy from distraction. Keep our hearts focused on You and on each other above all else. Amen.

Day Thirty Four

Reconnecting After Distance

Scripture: *Joel 2:25 (ESV) — "I will restore to you the years that the swarming locust has eaten."*

It had been a long winter, not just outside, but between Scott and Tara. The warmth that once filled their home had grown cold, replaced by short answers, missed glances, and the quiet weight of things left unsaid. They still shared a house, meals, and chores, but their hearts felt miles apart.

Neither could point to a single moment when the distance began. It had crept in slowly, through the exhaustion of parenting, the stress of bills, and the slow fade of intentional time together. What once felt easy now felt strained.

One evening, after putting the kids to bed, Tara sat at the kitchen table, flipping through an old photo album. Scott walked in and paused behind her, looking over her shoulder at a picture of them laughing on a beach during their first anniversary trip.

'We used to be so close,' Tara said quietly, not looking up. 'I miss what we had.'

Scott pulled out a chair and sat beside her. 'I miss it too. I didn't think it would get this far... but I don't want to stay here.'

Tears welled up in Tara's eyes. 'Neither do I. I just don't know how to get back.'

Scott reached for her hand. 'Maybe we don't go back. Maybe we start again from here. With God leading this time.'

That night, they prayed together for the first time in months. It was awkward and tender, but real. They confessed the ways they had pulled away, the things they had allowed to come between them. They asked God not just to fix their marriage, but to renew it.

In the weeks that followed, they began rebuilding, slowly, intentionally. They scheduled time to talk without distractions. They forgave past hurts. They laughed again, even if it felt unfamiliar at first. They invited God into the middle of their mess, and in return, He began to breathe life into places that had grown dry.

Restoration didn't come all at once, but it came. Day by day, trust was rebuilt, intimacy rekindled and love rediscovered. Their story wasn't perfect, but it was being rewritten, not by their strength, but by God's grace.

And in the hands of the Restorer, even the quietest love can sing again.

> Every couple goes through seasons of distance, emotionally, spiritually, or physically. But God is a restorer. No matter how long it's been, He can breathe new life into love that's gone quiet.

Joel 2:25 offers one of the most hope-filled promises in Scripture: 'I will restore to you the years that the swarming locust has eaten.' This verse speaks directly to the heart of couples who feel like too much time has passed, too much damage has been done, or too much distance has settled in. But with God, no season is beyond redemption. He doesn't just patch things up, He renews, restores, and breathes fresh life into what feels forgotten or broken.

Scott and Tara's story is a beautiful reminder that distance in marriage doesn't always begin with a dramatic event. Often, it's the slow erosion caused by exhaustion, distraction, and unspoken disappointment. But just as the drift happens gradually, so too can restoration, one honest conversation at a time, one prayer at a time, one act of grace at a time.

Every couple will walk through seasons where love feels quieter, connection feels strained, or hope feels dim. But those seasons are not the end. Reconnection begins with humility, the willingness to admit where you've grown apart, and honesty, the courage to name what's been lost or neglected. When you invite God into that space, you're not just asking Him to fix what's broken, but to make something new.

Restoration rarely happens overnight. It takes time, patience, and intentionality. But when grace leads the way, healing follows. Forgiveness becomes possible. Intimacy is rekindled. Trust is rebuilt. And slowly, the love that once felt distant begins to feel alive again. Reconnection starts with humility and honesty: naming where you've grown apart, asking forgiveness, and inviting God to rebuild what's been lost.

God's promise isn't just about recovering what was, it's about receiving something even deeper. A love that has been through winter and still chooses to bloom again is stronger, richer, and more rooted in grace. So if your marriage feels dry or disconnected, take heart. In the hands of the Restorer, even the quietest love can sing again.

God's promise isn't just to fix — it's to renew.

Reflection Question:
Where do you need God's restoring power to bring you close again?

Couples Challenge:
Plan one intentional "reconnection moment" this week, a slow dinner, a prayer walk, or time to talk.

Prayer:
Jesus, thank You for being the restorer of what's been broken. Help us reconnect in heart and spirit through Your healing grace. Amen.

Day Thirty Five

Unity That Glorifies God

Scripture: *John 17:22–23 (ESV) — "The glory that you have given me I have given to them, that they may be one even as we are one."*

Elizabeth and Carman had always been different. She was spontaneous and expressive; he was thoughtful and steady. In the early years of their marriage, those differences felt exciting, like puzzle pieces fitting together. But over time, what once drew them together began to create friction. Misunderstandings became more frequent, and conversations often ended in silence or frustration.

One evening, after an agitated discussion about parenting decisions, Elizabeth sat alone on the porch, tears sliding down her cheeks. She felt exhausted, not just from the argument, but from the weight of trying to make things work. Carman joined her a few minutes later, sitting quietly beside her.

After a long pause, he said, 'I know we don't always see things the same way. But I don't want to keep pulling in different directions. I want us to be one team, not just for us, but for something bigger.'

Elizabeth looked at him through tired eyes. 'I want that too. I just don't know how we get there when we keep clashing.'

Carman reached for her hand. 'Maybe it's not about agreeing on everything. Maybe it's about surrendering, not to each other's preferences, but to God's purpose for our marriage.'

They sat in silence, letting that truth settle between them. That night, they prayed together, not for the other person to change, but for their hearts to be united in purpose. They asked God to help them reflect His love, not just in the easy moments, but in the hard ones too.

Over time, their differences didn't disappear; they stopped being weapons and became strengths. Elizabeth's passion brought life to their home; Carman's steadiness brought peace. They learned to listen with humility, to forgive quickly, and to speak with grace.

Their unity wasn't perfect, but it was intentional. And as they continued to choose each other daily, through missteps, messes, and moments of joy, their marriage began to shine with something deeper than happiness. It reflected the glory of the God who had made them one.

And in that oneness, others saw not just a strong couple, but a glimpse of Christ's love.

Your unity as a couple is meant to display God's glory. When your marriage reflects peace, humility, and grace, the world gets a glimpse of Christ and His church.

John 17:22–23 offers a detailed glimpse into the heart of Jesus, His desire for unity among His followers, a unity that mirrors the oneness He shares with the Father. When applied to marriage, this passage reveals a powerful truth: our unity as a couple is not just for our benefit, but for God's glory. When a husband and wife walk in peace, humility, and grace, their relationship becomes a living testimony of Carman's love for His church.

Elizabeth and Carman's story remind us that unity doesn't mean sameness. God designed each spouse with unique strengths, personalities, and perspectives. The goal is not to erase those differences, but to bring them into harmony under His purpose. In marriage, oneness is not achieved by always agreeing, but by always choosing each other, especially in the moments when agreement is hard.

True unity is not passive; it is intentional. It's built through daily decisions to listen with empathy, to forgive without keeping score, and to serve without demanding in return. It's about surrender, not just to one another, but to the greater purpose God has for your marriage. When both partners lay down their pride and pick up grace, something holy begins to form.

Oneness in marriage is not about perfection; it's about persistence. It's about staying committed even when emotions waver. It's about choosing to fight for each other, not with each other. And when you pursue unity not just for your own happiness, but for God's glory, your love becomes a reflection of something eternal, a covenant that points the world to Christ.

So, if your marriage feels divided or strained, remember this: unity is not something you stumble into, it's something you build, one surrendered moment at a time. And as you do, your love will not only grow stronger, but it will also shine brighter, showing others the beauty of a God who makes two into one.

When you pursue oneness for God's glory, not just your happiness, your love becomes unshakable.

Reflection Question:
How can your marriage reflect God's glory more intentionally in this season?

Couples Challenge:
Together, pray a prayer of dedication offering your marriage again as a living testimony of God's love.

Prayer:
Father, make our marriage a reflection of Your glory. Unite us in purpose and fill our love with the beauty of Your presence. Amen.

WEEK SIX

DAYS 36-42

THEME:

CONFLICT & FORGIVENESS: TURNING
TENSION INTO TRANSFORMATION

KEY VERSE: EPHESIANS 4:31

Let all bitterness and wrath and anger and
clamor and slander be put away from you,
along with all malice

DAY THIRTY SIX

Seeing Conflict as Opportunity

Scripture: *James 1:19–20 (ESV)* — *"Let every person be quick to hear, slow to speak, slow to anger; for the anger of man does not produce the righteousness of God."*

It was their third year of marriage, and Bonnie had just finished cleaning up the dinner dishes when she noticed the trash still overflowing. Again.

She sighed, her shoulders tense. 'How many times do I have to remind him?' she muttered under her breath. When Shane walked into the kitchen, she didn't wait.

'You said you'd take out the trash. It's been sitting there all day,' she snapped.

Shane paused, surprised by the sharpness in her tone. He opened his mouth to defend himself, but something in him whispered, 'Wait.'

Instead of reacting, he leaned against the counter and looked at her. Really looked.

Bonnie's eyes were tired, and her words, though harsh, came from a place deeper than garbage. Shane took a breath. 'You're right,' he said quietly. 'I forgot. I'm sorry. Long day. But I should've remembered.'

Bonnie blinked. She had expected a retort, maybe a sarcastic comment. But his calm response disarmed her.

'I'm sorry too,' she said, her voice softer. 'I didn't mean to snap. I've just been feeling like I'm doing everything alone lately.'

Shane walked over and put his arms around her. 'Let's talk about it,' he said. 'I don't want you to feel that way.'

That night, the trash got taken out, but more importantly, so did the tension. Not because they avoided conflict, but because they chose to listen, wait, and let grace do the talking.

Over time, their marriage grew stronger. In that moment, conflict wasn't a wall between them. It became a doorway. A place where God met them, not to fix their flaws, but to teach them how to love more like Him.

Conflict isn't proof that love has failed; it's proof that two people are still growing. When handled God's way, it becomes a doorway to maturity and deeper understanding.

James 1:19–20 calls us to a higher way of responding in moments of tension: 'Let every person be quick to hear, slow to speak, slow to anger; for the anger of man does not produce the righteousness of God.' These words are not just general wisdom, they are a lifeline for relationships, especially in marriage. Conflict is inevitable, but how we handle it determines whether it becomes a wedge or a bridge.

Bonnie and Shane's story shows how quickly minor frustrations can escalate when left unchecked. But it also reveals the power of pausing, listening, and responding with grace. Shane's decision to be slow to speak and slow to anger didn't just defuse the moment, it opened the door for a deeper conversation and emotional connection. It turned a potential argument into an opportunity for growth.

> Conflict isn't proof that love is broken; it's proof that two people are still learning how to love well. Every disagreement is a chance to grow in humility, patience, and understanding. The goal in marriage isn't to avoid conflict altogether, that's unrealistic. Instead, it's to approach conflict in a way that honors God and each other.

When you choose to listen first, to pause before reacting, and to invite the Holy Spirit into the moment, conflict becomes a classroom. It teaches you how to extend grace, communicate with kindness, and see beyond surface issues to your spouse's deeper needs.

Marriage doesn't grow stronger through perfection — it grows stronger through grace-filled moments like these. So, the next time tension rises, remember you don't have to win the argument. You can win each other's hearts instead. Let love lead, let grace speak, and let every conflict become a doorway to deeper unity.

The goal isn't to avoid disagreements but to approach them with humility and patience. Listening first, pausing before reacting, and inviting the Holy Spirit to lead transforms conflict from a battlefield into a classroom for grace.

Reflection Question:

How can you approach your next disagreement as an opportunity to grow closer instead of to win?

Couples Challenge:

Before the next tough talk, pray together and ask God to help you listen before speaking.

Prayer:

Lord, teach us to see conflict as a place where You refine us. Give us patience, gentleness, and understanding hearts. Amen.

Day Thirty Seven

Rooting Out Pride

Scripture: *Proverbs 16:18 (ESV) — "Pride goes before destruction, and a haughty spirit before a fall."*

It had been two days since Martin and Lisa had spoken more than a few words to each other. The silence in their home was louder than any argument they had ever had. It all started with something small, Martin forgot to pick up the dry cleaning on his way home. Lisa, already feeling overwhelmed with work and the kids, had snapped. Martin responded with sarcasm, and from there, the tension grew.

Neither of them wanted to be the first to apologize.

Martin sat in the living room, scrolling through his phone, pretending not to notice the quiet. His heart was heavy, but his pride was louder. He kept thinking, 'She should say something first. She overreacted.'

In the other room, Lisa folded laundry in silence, her mind racing with similar thoughts. 'He never admits when he's wrong. Why should I go first?'

That night, they went to bed back-to-back, each hoping the other would break the silence. But the next morning, something shifted. As Martin was pouring his coffee, he looked over at Lisa standing by the sink. She looked tired, not just physically, but emotionally. He remembered how Jesus humbled Himself, even when He was right. And in that moment, Martin knew what he had to do.

He walked over, gently placed his hand on her shoulder, and said, 'I'm sorry. I was wrong to speak to you that way. I let my pride get in the way, and I don't want that between us.'

Lisa turned, surprised. Her eyes softened. 'Thank you,' she whispered. 'I'm sorry too. I let my frustration take over, and I didn't handle it well.'

That morning, the walls came down, not because someone won the argument, but because someone chose humility over pride. In that simple exchange, trust was rebuilt, and peace returned.

Marriage isn't about keeping score. It's about choosing to love over ego, grace over being right. When pride steps aside, love has room to grow.

Pride is the silent killer of peace. It refuses to apologize, insists on being right, and keeps score. In marriage, pride builds walls that love can't climb.

Proverbs 16:18 warns us with clarity: 'Pride goes before destruction, and a haughty spirit before a fall.' In marriage, pride doesn't always show up as loud arrogance, more often, it appears in the quiet refusal to say, 'I'm sorry,' the stubborn insistence on being right, or the silent treatment that stretches into days. It's subtle, but its effects are devastating. Pride builds walls that love cannot climb.

Martin and Lisa's story is a familiar one. A slight misstep, a sharp word, and suddenly, the air is thick with tension. But what truly deepens the divide isn't the original mistake — it's the pride that follows. When both spouses wait for the other to make the first move, reconciliation stalls. But when one chooses humility, healing begins.

> Marriage isn't about keeping score or proving who was right. It's about choosing to love over ego and grace over self-justification. Pride insists on fairness; love chooses forgiveness. Pride demands an apology; humility offers one first. When Martin remembered how Jesus humbled Himself, even when He was blameless, he found the strength to do the same. And in that moment, love won.

Jesus modeled a better way. Philippians 2 tells us that though He was equal with God, He emptied Himself and took the form of a servant. That kind of humility is the foundation of every strong marriage. When we let go of our need to win or be right, we create space for trust to grow and peace to return.

Admitting wrong doesn't weaken your position — it strengthens your relationship. It tells your spouse, 'You matter more to me than my pride.' And when both partners embrace that posture, even the deepest wounds can be healed.

If pride has crept into your relationship, don't wait for the other person to move first. Be the one who chooses humility. Because when pride steps aside, love has room to grow.

Jesus showed us a better way, He humbled Himself, even to the cross. When you choose humility, you make space for reconciliation. Admitting wrong doesn't weaken you; it strengthens trust.

Reflection Question:
Where does pride show up most in your relationship, and what would humility look like instead?

Couples Challenge:
Each of you name one area where you can practice humility this week (e.g., admitting fault, releasing control).

Prayer:
Father, free us from pride. Clothe us with humility that heals and draws us back together. Amen.

Day Thirty Eight

The Power of Gentle Response

Scripture: *Proverbs 15:18 (ESV) — "A hot-tempered man stirs up strife, but he who is slow to anger quiets contention."*

It was a Saturday morning, and the house was buzzing with the usual weekend chaos. The kids were loud, the laundry pile was growing, and the dishwasher had just decided to stop working. In the middle of it all, Tonya noticed that Paul had left his muddy shoes right in the entryway, again.

She felt the irritation rise. It wasn't just about the shoes; it was the fifth time that week she had picked up after him. She stormed into the living room where he was watching a game and opened her mouth, ready to let him have it.

But something stopped her.

She remembered the last time she snapped. He had shut down, barely said a word, and the rest of the day had been tense and distant. This time, she took a breath. She whispered a prayer under her breath and softened her voice.

'Hey, hunny,' she said gently, 'I know it's been a long week, but would you mind putting your shoes away? I've been trying to keep the floors clean, and it's been a bit overwhelming.'

Paul looked up, surprised, not by the request, but by the kindness in her tone. He turned off the TV and stood up.

'You're right. I'm sorry. I'll take care of it now,' he said, walking toward the shoes.

Tonya smiled, a little amazed. The same request, spoken with gentleness, had opened a door rather than built a wall.

That day, they moved through their chores together with more laughter than tension. The problems didn't disappear, but their hearts stayed connected.

Tone often matters more than truth. Even a right point can wound when spoken harshly. Gentleness disarms defensiveness; it opens the heart to hear.

Proverbs 15:18 says, 'A hot-tempered man stirs up strife, but he who is slow to anger quiets contention.' This simple yet powerful truth can make all the difference in marriage. In the heat of frustration, it's easy to believe that raising our voice or speaking sharply will get our point across. But more often, it only builds walls and hardens hearts.

Tonya and Paul's story show how tone can shift the entire atmosphere of a home. The issue was real, muddy shoes, repeated frustration, but the way Tonya chose to respond made all the difference. Instead of reacting with irritation, she paused, prayed, and chose gentleness. Her soft answer didn't just get the shoes picked up — it protected their connection.

> In marriage, it's not just what you say, but how you say it. A gentle voice can carry truth further than a loud one ever will. Gentleness doesn't mean weakness, it means choosing to love even when frustration feels justified. It's strength under control.

Tone often matters more than truth. You can be entirely correct and still cause harm if your words are wrapped in anger or sarcasm. Harshness stirs up defensiveness and division, but gentleness disarms and invites understanding. It opens the heart to listen, to respond, and to grow.

When tempers flare or irritation rises, take a breath. Whisper a prayer. Ask the Holy Spirit to guide your words. A soft answer doesn't mean avoiding truth, it means delivering it in a way that honors God and values your spouse.

Gentleness is a fruit of the Spirit, and when it shows up in our marriages, it creates space for peace, connection, and healing. So, the next time you feel the urge to snap, remember: a soft answer isn't weakness — it's wisdom. And it just might be the key to turning away wrath and drawing your spouse closer.

When tempers flare, pause. Take a breath, whisper a prayer, and answer softly. Gentleness is not weakness, it's strength under control, guided by love.

Reflection Question:

How can you bring more gentleness into your words and reactions?

Couples Challenge:

Agree on a simple signal or phrase to use when a conversation starts to get heated, your cue to pause and reset.

Prayer:

Lord, make our words soft and our hearts calm. Let gentleness lead every hard conversation. Amen.

Day Thirty Nine

Owning Your Part

Scripture: *Matthew 7:5 (ESV) — "First take the log out of your own eye, and then you will see clearly to take the speck out of your brother's eye."*

It started with a disagreement over something small, how to discipline their daughter after she talked back at dinner. Crystal thought they needed to be firm; Wes thought they needed to show more grace. Voices rose, frustration flared, and by the end of the evening, they were barely speaking.

The next morning, Crystal sat at the kitchen table with her coffee, replaying the argument in her mind. She felt justified. She believed she was right. But as she prayed, a quiet conviction settled in her heart. She remembered how quickly she had pointed out Wes's flaws, how she had accused instead of listening.

She looked up as Wes walked into the kitchen, still guarded, still hurt. She stood up and met his eyes.

'I've been thinking about last night,' she said softly. 'And I need to say I'm sorry. I was too quick to blame and didn't take time to understand your perspective. I didn't handle it the way I should have.'

Wes's shoulders relaxed. He hadn't expected that. He had spent the night building his own list of her faults, but her humility disarmed him.

'Thank you for saying that' he said. 'I'm sorry too. I could've listened better and not shut you down.'

That morning, they began working on their parenting dilemma, and took a step toward each other, not by proving who was right, but by owning their part in the wrong.

In marriage, healing often begins not with fixing the other person, but with looking inward. When one person chooses humility, it creates space for both spouses to grow. Grace flows most freely when blame is laid down and responsibility is picked up.

Blame blocks growth. Taking responsibility invites grace. Taking ownership of your part in conflict, even a small one, breaks the cycle of defensiveness and opens the way for healing.

Matthew 7:5 reminds us of a powerful principle that can transform the way we approach conflict in marriage: 'First take the log out of your own eye, and then you will see clearly to take the speck out of your brother's eye.' In the context of a relationship, this means that healing and understanding often begin not by pointing fingers, but by examining our own hearts first.

Crystal and Wes's story is a clear example of this. Their disagreement wasn't about a significant issue, it was a parenting decision, but the way they handled it created distance between them. Like many couples, both felt justified in their stance. But it wasn't until Crystal paused to reflect and took ownership of her part that the atmosphere began to shift. Her humility opened the door for Wes to lower his defenses and do the same.

In marriage, it's easy to focus on what the other person did wrong, to list their faults, replay their tone, or dwell on their mistakes. But blame blocks growth. It fuels defensiveness and keeps hearts at a distance. On the other hand, taking responsibility, even for just your part, invites grace into the conversation. It disarms pride and makes space for healing.

When one spouse chooses humility, it doesn't make them weak — it makes them like Christ. Jesus, who was blameless, chose to bear our faults so that we could be reconciled. When you admit fault first, even when you feel justified, you reflect that same humility. You remind your spouse that grace, not pride, rules your home.

You may not resolve every disagreement in one conversation, but you can always take a step toward unity. That step often begins with looking inward, laying down blame, and taking responsibility. And when you do, you'll find that healing follows humility, and grace has room to grow.

When you admit fault first, you reflect Christ's humility and remind your spouse that grace still rules your home.

Reflection Question:

What do you tend to justify instead of confess during conflict?

Couples Challenge:

During your next disagreement, each of you start by acknowledging one way you may have contributed.

Prayer:

Jesus, give us the courage to own our faults. Use honesty to rebuild trust between us. Amen.

DAY FORTY

Forgiving From the Heart

Scripture: *Colossians 3:13 (ESV) — "As the Lord has forgiven you, so you also must forgive."*

It had been almost a year since the betrayal. Nothing earth-shattering in the eyes of the world, just a secret credit card Justin had opened without telling Krista. He had racked up debt trying to cover some unexpected expenses, too embarrassed to admit they were struggling. When Krista found out, she felt blindsided. Trust, once solid, suddenly felt fragile.

They had talked it through, gone to counseling, and even made a plan to pay off the debt. But still, every time Justin made a purchase or mentioned money, Krista felt a twinge of resentment. She said she had forgiven him, but the weight of it still lingered in her heart.

One evening, as they sat on the porch watching their kids play in the yard, Justin reached for her hand.

'I know I hurt you,' he said quietly. 'And I can't undo what I did. But I want to thank you for staying. For giving me a second chance.'

Krista looked at him, her eyes filling with tears. She had been holding on to the pain like a shield, afraid that fully forgiving would mean forgetting. But in that moment, she realized forgiveness wasn't about pretending it didn't happen. It was about choosing to let it go so it wouldn't keep happening in her heart.

'I haven't always done it well,' she admitted. 'But I want to keep choosing to forgive. Not because it was okay, but because I love you more than I hate what happened.'

Justin squeezed her hand, and for the first time in a long time, the air between them felt lighter.

Forgiveness won't erase the past, but it will open the door to a future where grace can grow. In marriage, forgiveness isn't a one-time moment, it's a daily decision to love like Jesus, to release what could divide and cling to what can heal.

Forgiveness is the heartbeat of every lasting marriage. It doesn't erase pain, but it releases its control. Unforgiveness poisons intimacy; forgiveness purifies it.

Colossians 3:13 says, 'As the Lord has forgiven you, so you also must forgive.' This verse doesn't just offer a suggestion — it gives a command rooted in the very heart of the gospel. In marriage, where two imperfect people are learning to love each other through every season, forgiveness isn't optional. It's essential.

Justin and Krista's story is a reminder that forgiveness is rarely easy, especially when trust has been broken. Even after apologies are made and plans are set in motion, the emotional weight can linger. Krista said she had forgiven Justin, but the pain still echoed in her heart. That's the reality many couples face, saying the words is one thing; living them out is another.

Forgiveness doesn't erase the past. It doesn't mean forgetting or pretending it didn't hurt. What it does is release the offense from having ongoing power over your heart. Forgiveness is not about excusing the wrong, it's about choosing freedom over resentment. When Krista chose to keep forgiving, she wasn't ignoring the betrayal. She was refusing to let it define their future.

> In marriage, forgiveness is the heartbeat of intimacy. Unforgiveness poisons closeness, breeding suspicion and bitterness. But forgiveness purifies, making room for grace, trust, and healing to take root again. It's not a one-time act. It's a daily decision to walk in grace, to remember how much we've been forgiven by Christ, and to extend that same mercy to the one we've vowed to love.

When you forgive your spouse, you're not saying, 'It's okay.' You're saying, 'I won't let this wound keep wounding us.' You're choosing to move forward, hand in hand, even if the journey includes some scars. And in that choice, you reflect the very love of Jesus, the kind that covers, restores, and makes all things new.

Just as Christ forgave us completely, we're called to forgive continually. It's not a one-time event but a daily decision to walk in grace.

Reflection Question:

Who or what do you still need to release in forgiveness entirely, from the heart?

Couples Challenge:

Write a short prayer of forgiveness together for any lingering hurts, then read it aloud to God.

Prayer:

Lord, thank You for forgiving us fully. Please help us extend that same mercy to each other. Heal our hearts and renew our love. Amen.

DAY FORTY ONE

Healing Through Grace

Scripture: *Psalm 147:3 (ESV) — "He heals the brokenhearted and binds up their wounds."*

It had been a hard season. Between the stress of caring for her aging mother and the long hours at work, Naomi had little left to give. Derrick, her husband, tried to be supportive, but his own frustration grew as their connection faded into silence and short tempers.

One evening, after another quiet dinner filled with unspoken tension, Naomi stood at the sink washing dishes. Derrick approached, unsure of what to say. Weeks of miscommunication had left both of them bruised, hearts tender from words that had missed the mark.

He finally spoke, his voice low and hesitant.

'Naomi, I know I haven't been what you needed lately. I've been impatient and distant. I miss us.'

She didn't answer right away. Her hands stayed in the soapy water, but her heart stirred. She had been waiting for him to see her pain, but she hadn't seen his either.

She turned to face him, eyes misty.

'I'm hurting, Derrick. But I know you are too. I don't want us to keep walking around each other like strangers.'

He reached out, gently taking her still-damp hand, which was holding a dish towel.

'Let's start again,' he said. 'Not by pretending it didn't hurt, but by letting grace start to heal it.'

That night, they sat close on the couch, talked softly, and prayed together for the first time in weeks. It wasn't a breakthrough moment, but it was a beginning.

Healing didn't come all at once. It came in small choices, kind words, patient pauses, gentle touches. Grace became the balm that softened the soreness and slowly rekindled the warmth between them.

The Holy Spirit doesn't rush healing, He walks with us through it, mending what conflict has bruised, and breathing life into what felt lost.

Psalm 147:3 says, 'He heals the brokenhearted and binds up their wounds.' This verse is a tender reminder that God doesn't ignore our pain — He meets us in it. In marriage, there will be seasons when both spouses are hurting, when misunderstandings pile up, and emotional distance grows. But even in those moments, healing is possible, not through quick fixes, but through grace-filled steps toward one another.

Naomi and Derrick's story reflect the quiet ache that can settle in a relationship when life becomes overwhelming. Their pain wasn't caused by betrayal or a single major event, it was the slow erosion of connection under the weight of stress, fatigue, and unmet expectations. But what made the difference was their willingness to acknowledge the hurt and invite grace into the space between them.

> In marriage, pain is sometimes inevitable, but so is restoration when love leans on grace. Healing doesn't always come in dramatic moments. Often, it begins with a soft word, a sincere apology, or a simple prayer whispered together. When we allow the Holy Spirit to guide us, He doesn't rush the process, He gently walks with us, mending what conflict has bruised and breathing life into what felt lost.

Grace is the gentle balm that softens hardened hearts and heals what conflict has bruised. When words have cut deep or actions have hurt, God's grace can still restore tenderness. It doesn't erase the past, but it makes room for the future. When words have cut deep or actions have disappointed, grace says, 'Let's begin again.' And when both spouses choose to keep showing up with kindness, patience, and humility, healing begins to take root.

Love anchored in grace never stops reaching. It's not about pretending everything is fine, it's about choosing to stay tender, even when things have been tense. So, if your marriage feels bruised or distant, take heart. The God who binds up wounds is still at work. Keep inviting Him into the process. Healing may take time, but with grace, it's always possible.

Keep inviting the Holy Spirit to soothe what's sore and rekindle what's dim.

Reflection Question:

What wound still needs God's healing touch in your relationship?

Couples Challenge:

Pray over that area together, asking God for emotional and relational healing.

Prayer:

Jesus, we invite Your healing grace into every hurt. Bind our hearts together again in peace and mercy. Amen.

DAY FORTY TWO

Moving Forward Together

Scripture: *Philippians 3:13–14 (ESV) — "Forgetting what lies behind and straining forward to what lies ahead, I press on toward the goal."*

It had been a long road for Jeff and Monica. A year earlier, their marriage nearly crumbled under the weight of unspoken resentment and emotional distance. Harsh words were exchanged, trust was cracked, and for a while, they lived more like roommates than partners. But through counseling, prayer, and a willingness to forgive, they began to rebuild.

Now, on a quiet Sunday afternoon, Jeff and Monica sat on their back porch, sipping coffee. The sun was warm, and the breeze carried the sound of their kids laughing in the yard. It should have been peaceful, but Monica's mind kept drifting back to the past, the arguments, the nights spent in tears, the silence that once filled this very space.

Jeff noticed her distant gaze. He reached over and gently took her hand.

'You're thinking about it again, aren't you?' he asked.

Monica nodded. 'Sometimes it still sneaks up on me. I know we've forgiven each other, but part of me is afraid of going back.'

Jeff squeezed her hand. 'We're not going back. We've already walked through the fire. But we can't keep living in the smoke.'

Monica looked at him, surprised by the clarity in his words.

'God didn't bring us this far just to keep us looking behind,' he continued. 'We've been given a second chance, not just to survive, but to grow. I don't want to keep reliving what broke us. I want to start building what's ahead.'

Tears welled in Monica's eyes, not from pain this time, but from hope. She leaned her head on his shoulder and whispered, 'Then let's move forward. Together.'

That day, they didn't just remember their healing, they stepped into a new chapter. They started dreaming again, planning a weekend getaway, talking about ways to serve together at church, and even laughing about things that once would have sparked tension.

Forgiveness had opened the door, but now it was time to walk through it. Not to forget the past, but to stop letting it define them. With grace behind them and God before them, they pressed on, hand in hand, toward something better than they had before.

In marriage, healing is a beginning, not an end. And with Christ, there is always more ahead than what lies behind. Once grace has done its work, it's time to move forward with renewed purpose and unity.

Philippians 3:13–14 reminds us that in Christ, our direction matters more than our history: 'Forgetting what lies behind and straining forward to what lies ahead, I press on toward the goal.' This passage speaks deeply into the journey of marriage, especially for couples who have walked through hurt, healing, and the long road of rebuilding trust.

Jeff and Monica's story is a powerful picture of what it means to move forward. Their marriage had been fractured but not finished. Forgiveness opened the door to restoration, but it was their willingness to stop living in the shadow of the past that allowed them to truly step into a new chapter.

In marriage, healing is not the end of the story, it's the beginning of a new one. When forgiveness has been given and grace has done its work, the next step is to press forward. That doesn't mean pretending the past didn't happen. It means refusing to let it define the future. Holding on to old wounds, even after forgiveness, keeps couples stuck in cycles of fear and regret. But when you choose to fix your eyes on what God is building ahead, you begin to walk in freedom.

> Forgiveness is not the finish line — it's the starting point for a new season. It's where damaged trust begins to be rebuilt, where hope is rekindled, and where purpose is rediscovered. God doesn't just want to repair your marriage, He wants to renew it, to give it fresh vision, deeper intimacy, and greater strength than before.

Don't keep replaying old wounds. Let go of what lies behind and press on together toward what lies ahead. God has new ground for your marriage to claim, new joy, new peace, and new opportunities to serve and grow together. With grace behind you and Christ before you, the best is not behind you. It's still to come. Keep pressing forward, hand in hand.

Reflection Question:
What new chapter do you sense God inviting you into as a couple?

Couples Challenge:
Write down one shared goal or prayer for your marriage's next season and post it where you'll see it daily.

Prayer:
Father, thank You for bringing us through. Help us move forward in grace, vision, and unity. Use our story to glorify You. Amen.

About the Author

Daniel Moore has called Neosho, Missouri home his whole life. He's been married to his wife, Michelle, for over 20 years, and together they've built a full and busy life with three (now adult) children, two of them which have awesome spouses, two dogs, and now four granddaughters who keep them smiling. Daniel and Michelle host the podcast *Marriage Life and More*, where they share weekly conversations about God's design for marriage. Daniel also hosts *Connecting the Gap*, a Bible study podcast that helps listeners dig deeper into Scripture. When he's not working at a Christian radio station or running his computer business, you can usually find him out on a bike ride, kayaking, catching a football game, or just spending time with Michelle, the thing he enjoys most of all!

You Can Connect with us at:

https://www.marriagelifeandmore.com

https://www.connectingthegap.net

https://x.com/ctgaponline

https://www.facebook.com/ctgaponline/

https://www.instagram.com/ctgaponline/

Also Available

Connecting the Gap Ministries

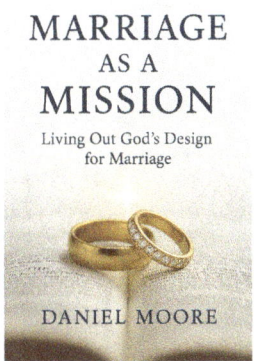

MARRIAGE AS A MISSION
Living Out God's Design for Marriage

DANIEL MOORE

This book is a Christ-centered guide that redefines marriage not just as a relationship, but as a divine calling. Rooted in biblical truth, this book explores God's original intent for marriage and offers practical wisdom for couples seeking to grow in love, unity, and purpose. Through topics such as covenant commitment, spiritual intimacy, servant-hearted leadership, and shared ministry, readers are invited to see their marriage as a powerful expression of the gospel. Whether you're newlyweds or seasoned partners, this book will inspire you to embrace your marriage as a mission and experience deeper fulfillment through Christ.

This is available in paperback, hardback, and Kindle on Amazon.com. http://bit.ly/4n Ms7kP

It is also available at our website at www.marriagelifeandmore.com.

The e-book is also available on Google Play Books and Apple Books.

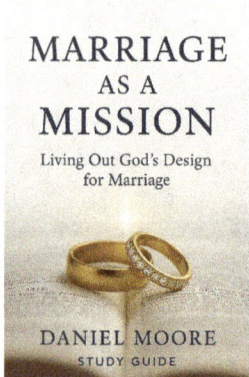

This study guide is a companion to *Marriage as a Mission – Living Out God's Design for Marriage*, designed to help couples and small groups dive deeper into God's purpose for marriage. Each section offers thought-provoking questions, practical exercises, and biblical insights that guide husbands and wives toward a Christ-centered relationship. Whether used individually, as a couple, or in a group setting, this guide will help you apply God's Word to real-life situations and strengthen your marriage as a reflection of His love and mission in the world.

This study guide is available in paperback format on Amazon only. http://bit.ly/4nac67e

www.ingramcontent.com/pod-product-compliance
Lightning Source LLC
Chambersburg PA
CBHW070716130626
46553CB00005B/2010